Tutor Master Services

David Malindine

B.A.(Hons), M.A.(London), P.G.C.E.,
Adv.Dip.Ed.(Open), R.S.A. Cert.

Tutor Master Services
61 Ashness Gardens
Greenford
Middlesex
UB6 0RW

david@tutormaster-services.co.uk
www.tutormaster-services.co.uk

Acknowledgements

Thanks to Christine Malindine for preparing this book
and to Martyn Clarke for proofreading the scripts

For
Evie and Ned

First Published 2014

ISBN: 978-0-9555909-6-2

Printed by G.H.Smith & Son, Design Printing Publishing, Easingwold, York
Tel: 01347 821329 Fax: 01347 822576
Web: www.ghsmith.com

Contents

Who this book is for

The ability to read and make meaning from written information are crucial skills for students of all ages. These skills are tested regularly in state, grammar and independent/private schools.

When children move from primary school to secondary school at the end of Year 6 aged 11 years, some parents may wish their child to take examinations in order to achieve a place at a grammar or independent/private school. Because the entry requirements to such schools vary from place to place around the country it is important for parents to prepare themselves by doing some research about the schools that they may wish their child to attend.

Schools publish their entry requirements for students moving schools at age 11+ and it is important that parents find out about the admissions policies of the school and any examinations that the school may set in order that they can prepare their children properly.

Examinations in English tend to be a reading passage accompanied by either a multiple choice or standard answer comprehension test, plus a piece of written creative writing, composition or essay.

For multiple choice answer tests, answers are recorded by ticking or marking a box on an answer sheet. For standard comprehension tests answers are written in an answer book.

It is my experience as a tutor that many parents enter children for more than one type of school. The Tutor Master papers take this into account by providing separate books with practice tests for both Multiple Choice English Comprehension and Standard English Comprehension papers.

This book has been written with the aim of helping students practise their comprehension skills as a way of improving their abilities to understand written information.

The tests contained in this book have been prepared for children in school years 4, 5 and 6, ages 8 – 11 years old. As well as being helpful for general revision and practice, these comprehension tests are written to assist particularly students who are preparing for entrance examinations at 11+ for grammar schools and independent schools.

How to use this book

This book contains important, practical advice on the best ways to approach multiple choice comprehension tests and how to write effective and purposeful answers. The book also provides tips and advice for writing composition/essays. These are writing tests that cover aspects of creative writing such as stories, reports and letters.

Five multiple choice comprehension tests are provided, each with a reading passage followed by questions that are answered by the students on the papers provided.

Each of the five comprehension tests is accompanied by a composition/essay test that provides a choice of two tasks for the student to attempt.

A clear, helpful and detailed mark scheme is provided for both the comprehension test and compositions to enable an accurate assessment to be made of each student's performance.

Tutor Master Services

ENGLISH
Comprehension

Multiple Choice

Tips and Advice
for completing
Comprehensions and Compositions

www.tutormaster-services.co.uk www.tutormaster-services.co.uk www.tutormaster-services.co.uk www.tutormaster-services.co.uk

Comprehension Tips for Multiple Choice

It is a good idea for the student to read through this advice with an adult before they begin the comprehension papers.

- Read the story passage carefully as it is important you understand it. Remember as much as you can. (It may help if you think of your brain as a sponge, soaking up as many details as you can!)
- Read the question carefully then check the reading passage to find the answer and then mark your answer in the box provided on the answer sheet.
- It is important that you understand that you are allowed to go back and check the reading passage to help you answer the questions. In fact it is **essential** to use the reading passage to help. This exam is not a memory test.
- If you are not sure what a word means in a question, go back to the passage and read the sentences that come before and after the word you need to explain. Use the **context** in which the word is used to have your best guess.
- Always try to mark an answer for every question. If you do not answer you will lose marks. Always have a guess if you are unsure as you never know, you may be correct!
- Be careful! Multiple choice comprehension tests may appear to be easier than they are. If you finish quickly use the full time to go back and check your answers again.
- Some questions are about grammar, spellings and Parts of Speech. To find out more about words and their meanings my book, *Tutor Master helps you Learn English - A Literacy Dictionary*, contains lots of helpful definitions and examples.

Practical Advice

- Agree a suitable time and place where the practice test will be carried out. It is advisable for the student to conduct the test in a place where they can be supervised and timed by an adult and which will also be free from noise or distractions.
- Provide a clock that the student can see, several pencils, a ruler and an eraser. It is probably better to write answers in pencil so that any mistakes can be more easily corrected.
- As this is a practice situation it is probably helpful to read through the instructions on the front page with the student before they begin.
- Make sure the student understands what they have to do before they begin and give them the chance to ask any questions.

Tips for Writing Compositions

These are general guidelines only. For more detailed advice and practical help with story writing, see *Tutor Master helps you Write Stories Book 1* and *Tutor Master helps you Write Stories Book 2*.

- When choosing a story to write in an exam it is a good idea to choose the title that you may be able to write from your own experience. This makes it easier as you know how the story begins, what happens and how it ends.
- It is **very important** to make sure that the story you write is about the title you have chosen or been given.
- Examiners often prefer you to show your writing skills by making your story sound true, even if it is made up. Amazing, improbable adventure stories are often difficult to complete in the half hour of writing time available.
- Try to think how your story will end **before** you start to write. It is very important that you finish the story. If you already know how it will end you can quickly bring it to a conclusion if you find you are running out of time.
- It is a good idea to write your stories in the **past tense** as you will find it easier to maintain this throughout the story.
- Make sure your story has a clear **beginning** where you set the scene and introduce the main ideas – this should be fairly short, maybe just one paragraph. Make sure the **middle** part of your story is the longest part containing two, three or more paragraphs. **End** your story with a fairly short concluding paragraph.
- Begin a new paragraph each time you change the topic you are writing about.
- Be careful to punctuate your work using the rules for punctuating written work.
- Be careful to spell correctly, especially those words you know you find difficult.
- Try to include some **direct speech** correctly punctuated using the rules for punctuating direct speech.
- Write good descriptions using adjectives, adverbs and similes.
- Try to describe your **feelings** or the **feelings** of the characters you are writing about.

Tutor Master Services

ENGLISH
Comprehension
Multiple Choice Introductory
Paper 2A

50 minutes

Read the following carefully:

1. You should read the passage and then answer the questions about it. It is a good idea to look back at the passage to check your answers as many times as you want. There are also some spelling, punctuation and grammar exercises to do.
2. This is a multiple-choice test. You need to mark your answer to each question on the answer sheet. You should mark only one answer for each question.
3. Draw a line clearly through the rectangle next to your answer. If you make a mistake, rub it out as fully as you can and mark in your new answer.
4. Mark your answer in the column that has the same number as the test question.
5. Try to do as many questions as you can. If you cannot do a question, move on to the next one. If you are not sure of an answer, have your best guess at the one you think may be correct.
6. Work as quickly and as carefully as you can.
7. You will have 50 minutes to do the comprehension and 30 minutes for the composition.

Published by:

Tutor Master Services, 61 Ashness Gardens, Greenford, Middlesex UB6 0RW.

ISBN: 978-0-9555909-6-2

www.tutormaster-services.co.uk www.tutormaster-services.co.uk www.tutormaster-services.co.uk www.tutormaster-services.co.uk

Read the passage below and answer the following questions carefully. It is a good idea to go back and check the passage to find your answers. Write your answers neatly on the answer sheet.

Aladdin

In a land far away to the East, there once lived a lazy lad named Aladdin. His father Qaseem had died of grief as his idle son made no attempt to mend his ways and lived as an impoverished ne'er-do-well.

One day a stranger visited the town where Aladdin lived and on meeting Aladdin announced that he was Aladdin's long lost Uncle Mustafa. Aladdin and his mother were taken aback at this news as it had long been thought that Uncle Mustafa had died, but their misgivings were put aside when the stranger convinced them of his goodwill by making arrangements to set up young Aladdin as a merchant.

The very next day Aladdin and Mustafa set off to buy stock to begin their trading venture. They journeyed for a long while through the mountains until they halted in a narrow valley. After lighting a fire Mustafa produced some magic powder which he threw into the flames and in a flash of sparks and smoke a stone slab was revealed, and set in it was a large brass ring. Mustafa pulled on the ring and the slab opened to reveal steps leading down to an underground cave filled with treasure. Mustafa promised Aladdin great wealth if he were to go down into the cave to retrieve an old oil lamp that would be found on an ancient stone table.

Aladdin was apprehensive at the thought of stepping down into the chamber but was eventually won over by his uncle who offered him a special ring for protection in case of trouble.

Once inside the cave Aladdin picked his way carefully through the piles of treasures until he found the lamp. Picking it up, he carefully retraced his way and climbed the steps. As he was nearing the top his uncle demanded the lamp, but as Aladdin was not yet safely out of the cave he refused. In a fit of anger Mustafa uttered some magic words, and the stone slab slammed shut. Aladdin was trapped.

Immediately Aladdin realised that Mustafa had tried to trick him and he was not his real uncle, but a wicked magician who had wanted to use Aladdin for his own ends. Alone in the cave, Aladdin clasped his hands together in prayer and as he did so inadvertently rubbed the ring given to him by the evil Mustafa. At once, a genie appeared who was able to grant Aladdin his wish to be saved, and took him home to his mother.

Once at home Aladdin's mother was desperate for food and money as they were very poor. Aladdin suggested that they sell the old lamp, but before he did so, decided to give it a quick polish. Instantly, a huge genie, more powerful than the first, appeared and informed them he was bound to do the bidding of the person in possession of the lamp.

With the aid of the genie of the lamp, Aladdin and his mother were able to

www.tutormaster-services.co.uk www.tutormaster-services.co.uk www.tutormaster-services.co.uk www.tutormaster-services.co.uk

become rich and powerful by selling silverware conjured up by the genie of the lamp. Eventually, wealthy and prosperous, Aladdin married Princess Badroulbadour, the Sultan's daughter, and with the help of the genie moved into a palace far more magnificent than that of the Sultan himself.

One day however, the sinister magician returned to the town and tricked Aladdin's wife, who was unaware of the lamp's importance, by offering to exchange "new lamps for old". Once in possession of the lamp he ordered the genie of the lamp to take the palace and the princess and magically transport them to his own city in a country far away.

Desperately sad, anxious and alone, Aladdin summoned the assistance of the genie of the ring. Although the genie of the ring had lesser power and was unable to undo the magic of the genie of the lamp, he was able to magically transport Aladdin to the site of his palace and to his wife the Princess Badroulbadour.

When she laid eyes on Aladdin again the princess was delighted to see him and reassured him of her love for him. She told him that the dishonourable magician had told her that Aladdin was long since dead and she should marry him now. Princess Badroulbadour had constantly refused him his wish and remained loyal to Aladdin.

To trick the evil magician, Aladdin and his princess hatched a cunning plan. They agreed that the princess would pretend to accept his marriage requests. One night as they prepared to celebrate the forthcoming wedding Princess Badroulbadour persuaded the magician to go down to the wine cellar to bring back some fine wines to drink.

Bedazzled by her beauty and charms, the magician hurried off. Meanwhile the princess sprinkled some special powder that Aladdin had provided, into a cup. On his return the magician poured out the wine and drank from the cup. Immediately, he fell down, quite dead!

Aladdin retrieved his magic lamp and asked the genie to restore things to the way they were. Soon the palace, with Aladdin and Princess Badroulbadour inside, was returned safely to the kingdom. The Sultan was overjoyed to see his daughter safely returned. Aladdin was reunited with his mother, and they all lived happily ever after.

Answer these questions carefully. It is a good idea to go back and check the passage to find your answers. You should choose the best answer and mark its letter on your answer sheet.

1. We are told that Qaseem died of grief as his son Aladdin was
   a) thoughtful
   b) resourceful
   c) industrious
   d) lazy
   e) thrifty
2. Aladdin and his mother were surprised to meet Uncle Mustafa as they thought he was
   a) abroad
   b) on holiday
   c) lost
   d) missing
   e) dead
3. Uncle Mustafa helped Aladdin find employment as a
   a) lamp maker
   b) relative
   c) merchant
   d) treasure hunter
   e) nephew
4. At first Aladdin and Mustafa set off in order to
   a) find a magic lamp
   b) purchase produce to buy and sell
   c) locate the cave of treasures
   d) trade in magic lamps
   e) get to know each other better
5. When they reached their destination the first thing Mustafa did was
   a) produce magic powder
   b) flash some sparks
   c) have a smoke
   d) rub a brass ring
   e) light a fire
6. The large brass ring was
   a) fixed in a lump of stone
   b) fixed on Mustafa's finger
   c) fixed on Aladdin's finger
   d) found in an underground cave
   e) flashing with sparks

7. To enter the underground cave, Aladdin would need to
   a) slide down a pole
   b) climb down a ladder
   c) go down in an elevator
   d) climb down some steps
   e) use the escalator

8. The thought of going down into the chamber made Aladdin feel
   a) confident
   b) optimistic
   c) uneasy
   d) hopeful
   e) certain

9. In order to persuade Aladdin to go into the cave, Mustafa
   a) offered magic words of protection
   b) provided a magic lamp to illuminate his way
   c) offered magic powder to drink as a potion
   d) provided a genie to accompany him
   e) gave him a special ring

10. Once inside the cave Aladdin found the lamp
   a) on a special altar made of gold
   b) on a pile of gold coins, lamps and rings
   c) in a treasure chest
   d) under a magic carpet
   e) on an old table made of stone

11. Aladdin refused to hand the magic lamp to Mustafa because
   a) he was off balance and might fall
   b) he feared for his safety
   c) his uncle demanded fiercely
   d) he wanted the lamp for himself
   e) he did not ask using the magic word

12. As he pressed his hands together Aladdin rubbed the magic ring
   a) intentionally
   b) unwillingly
   c) unintentionally
   d) deliberately
   e) knowingly

13. As a solution to their plight of hunger and poverty Aladdin and his mother decided to firstly
    a) set up a shop selling lighting by magical means
    b) ask a genie to provide wealth beyond their wildest dreams
    c) sell the magic ring
    d) sell the old lamp
    e) trade in the old lamp for a new one
14. Rubbing the magic lamp helped Aladdin and his mother
    a) improve their fortunes
    b) neglect their fortunes
    c) disprove their fortunes
    d) disregard their fortunes
    e) discredit their fortunes
15. We are led to believe that the "sinister magician" (line 43) is
    a) the genie of the ring
    b) Uncle Mustafa
    c) the genie of the lamp
    d) Badroulbadour
    e) the Sultan
16. One thing the genie of the ring could do to help Aladdin was
    a) exchange the magic ring for the magic lamp
    b) outperform the genie of the lamp when it came to feats of magic
    c) move him to visit Badroulbadour in Mustafa's palace
    d) call an urgent meeting of magicians of the Magic Circle
    e) magically transport him to a cave of fortune
17. The main thing that Mustafa longed to do was
    a) get rich quick
    b) find fame and fortune
    c) marry Aladdin's widowed mother
    d) live in a huge and majestic palace
    e) marry Princess Badroulbadour
18. The main reason why the principal characters lived happily ever after was because
    a) Aladdin repossessed the lamp and reacquainted with the genie
    b) Aladdin and Princess Badroulbadour were reunited
    c) the Sultan was very happy at the positive outcome
    d) Aladdin and his mother came together again
    e) Uncle Mustafa drank the poisoned potion

The following questions are about the meaning of words as they are used in the passage.

19. The word closest in meaning to the word 'misgivings' (line 7) is
    a) inclination
    b) suspicions
    c) decisions
    d) convictions
    e) considerations

20. The word that is most similar to 'revealed' (line 14) is
    a) hidden
    b) covered
    c) concealed
    d) displayed
    e) obscured

21. The word 'sinister' (line 43) informs us that the magician was
    a) innocent
    b) kindly
    c) menacing
    d) considerate
    e) compassionate

22. Another word for 'assistance' (line 48) could be
    a) hindrance
    b) aid
    c) restriction
    d) obstruction
    e) interference

23. The words, 'his' (line 67) and 'they' (line 68) are both examples of
    a) abstract nouns
    b) proper nouns
    c) pronouns
    d) adverbs
    e) verbs

These questions are about words and phrases as they are used in the passage.

24. The phrase "impoverished ne'er-do-well" (line 3) suggests Aladdin was
    a) wealthy, enterprising and industrious
    b) successful, aspirational and rich
    c) motivated, eager and affluent
    d) enthusiastic, determined and prosperous
    e) poverty stricken, idle and work-shy

25. The phrase, "he carefully retraced his way" (line 23-24) means Aladdin
    a) diligently walked back the way he came
    b) cautiously drew around his footprints
    c) meticulously made his way forward
    d) heedlessly walked backward
    e) recklessly made his return

26. The genie was "bound to do the bidding" (line 37-38) means he was
    a) obliged to pay some attention to
    b) likely to consider the options of
    c) compelled to obey the instructions of
    d) have regard to the request of
    e) consider the possibility of

27. The phrase "once in the possession of the lamp" (line 45) means that Mustafa
    a) released the lamp
    b) acquired the lamp
    c) relinquished the lamp
    d) discharged the lamp
    e) delivered the lamp

28. The phrase "hatched a cunning plan" (lines 58) tells us that Aladdin and Badroulbadour
    a) had a simple notion
    b) designed an honest plan
    c) conceived a straightforward conspiracy
    d) devised a sly plot
    e) developed an ordinary idea

Read the following passage. There are some *spelling* mistakes. On each numbered line there is either *one* mistake or *no* mistake. Find the group of words with the mistake in it and mark its letter on your answer sheet. *If there is no mistake, mark* X.

A Domestic Disaster

29. It was disarstar the day the television broke.

A	B	C	D	X
It was	disarstar the	day the	television broke.	

30. The children had fineshed their homework and were

A	B	C	D	X
The children	had fineshed	their homework	and were	

31. ready to enjoy their liesure time. As they

A	B	C	D	X
ready to	enjoy their	liesure time.	As they	

32. settled down to wacht, suddenly there was a huge

A	B	C	D	X
settled down	to wacht,	suddenly there	was a huge	

33. niose and the television erupted in smoke and fumes.

A	B	C	D	X
niose and	the television	erupted in	smoke and fumes.	

34. Everyone was disappointed and extremely frustrated that it

A	B	C	D	X
Everyone was	disappointed and	extremely frustrated	that it	

35. had happend at the very minute that their favourite

A	B	C	D	X
had happend	at the very	minute that	their favourite	

36. show was about to begin. It was all very frustrating.

A	B	C	D	X
show was	about to begin.	It was all	very frustrating.	

Read the following passage. There are some mistakes in the use of *capital letters* and *punctuation*. On each numbered line there is either *one* mistake or *no* mistake. Find the group of words with the mistake in it and mark its letter on your answer sheet. *If there is no mistake, mark* X.

Playing Outdoors

37. Evie and Ned went out into the garden to play

A	B	C	D	X
Evie and Ned	went out	into the	garden to play	

38. I'd like to play with the kite," said Evie.

A	B	C	D	X
I'd like to	play with	the kite,"	said Evie.	

39. No, lets play | on the swing," | replied Ned. | In the end

A	B	C	D	X

40. they decided | to get out. | the paddling pool. | As it was

A	B	C	D	X

41. a fine day, | they thought | theyd ask | their sister Lil

A	B	C	D	X

42. if she wanted | to join them | and have | fun in the

A	B	C	D	X

43. sun. However they | found that | shed' gone | out with her friend.

A	B	C	D	X

In each question you have to choose the *best word* or *group of words* to complete this passage so that it makes sense and is written in correct English. You should choose one of the five answers and mark its letter on your answer sheet.

The Birthday Treat

44. For his birthday Barnaby

ask	asking	asked	will ask	arsked
A	B	C	D	E

45. his parents if he would be

aloud	alowed	allowed	alloud	alowd
A	B	C	D	E

46. to ... his friends bowling.

take	tack	taking	taked	go
A	B	C	D	E

47. His mum and dad

agread	egreed	egread	agreed	could
A	B	C	D	E

48. with his idea and they ... out invitations.

send	sent	sented	sended	scent
A	B	C	D	E

49. Soon his friends ... and

reply	replyed	replieyed	repleid	replied
A	B	C	D	E

50. an ... day was enjoyed by all.

exiting	exicting	excited	exciting	excite
A	B	C	D	E

Answer Sheet

Mark your answer in the box with a line as shown using a pencil.
If you need to correct use a rubber to rub out. Do not cross out any change or make any other mark in the boxes.

Example	
a.	[ ]
b.	[ ]
c.	[—]
d.	[ ]
e.	[ ]

Q1.	Q2.	Q3.	Q4.	Q5.
a. [ ]	a. [ ]	a. [ ]	a. [ ]	a. [ ]
b. [ ]	b. [ ]	b. [ ]	b. [ ]	b. [ ]
c. [ ]	c. [ ]	c. [ ]	c. [ ]	c. [ ]
d. [ ]	d. [ ]	d. [ ]	d. [ ]	d. [ ]
e. [ ]	e. [ ]	e. [ ]	e. [ ]	e. [ ]

Q6.	Q7.	Q8.	Q9.	Q10.
a. [ ]	a. [ ]	a. [ ]	a. [ ]	a. [ ]
b. [ ]	b. [ ]	b. [ ]	b. [ ]	b. [ ]
c. [ ]	c. [ ]	c. [ ]	c. [ ]	c. [ ]
d. [ ]	d. [ ]	d. [ ]	d. [ ]	d. [ ]
e. [ ]	e. [ ]	e. [ ]	e. [ ]	e. [ ]

Q11.	Q12.	Q13.	Q14.	Q15.
a. [ ]	a. [ ]	a. [ ]	a. [ ]	a. [ ]
b. [ ]	b. [ ]	b. [ ]	b [ ]	b. [ ]
c. [ ]	c. [ ]	c. [ ]	c. [ ]	c. [ ]
d. [ ]	d. [ ]	d. [ ]	d. [ ]	d [ ]
e. [ ]	e. [ ]	e. [ ]	e [ ]	e. [ ]

Q16.	Q17.	Q18.	Q19.	Q20.
a. [ ]	a. [ ]	a. [ ]	a. [ ]	a. [ ]
b. [ ]	b. [ ]	b. [ ]	b. [ ]	b. [ ]
c. [ ]	c. [ ]	c. [ ]	c. [ ]	c. [ ]
d. [ ]	d. [ ]	d. [ ]	d. [ ]	d. [ ]
e. [ ]	e. [ ]	e. [ ]	e. [ ]	e. [ ]

Q21.	Q22.	Q23.	Q24.	Q25.
a. [ ]	a. [ ]	a. [ ]	a. [ ]	a. [ ]
b. [ ]	b. [ ]	b. [ ]	b. [ ]	b. [ ]
c. [ ]	c. [ ]	c. [ ]	c. [ ]	c. [ ]
d. [ ]	d. [ ]	d. [ ]	d. [ ]	d. [ ]
e. [ ]	e. [ ]	e. [ ]	e. [ ]	e. [ ]

Q26.	Q27.	Q28.
a. [ ]	a. [ ]	a. [ ]
b. [ ]	b. [ ]	b. [ ]
c. [ ]	c. [ ]	c. [ ]
d. [ ]	d. [ ]	d. [ ]
e. [ ]	e. [ ]	e. [ ]

Q29.	Q30.	Q31.	Q32.	Q33.
A. [ ]	A. [ ]	A. [ ]	A. [ ]	A. [ ]
B. [ ]	B. [ ]	B. [ ]	B. [ ]	B. [ ]
C. [ ]	C. [ ]	C. [ ]	C. [ ]	C. [ ]
D. [ ]	D. [ ]	D. [ ]	D. [ ]	D. [ ]
X. [ ]	X. [ ]	X. [ ]	X. [ ]	X. [ ]

Q34.	Q35.	Q36.	Q37.	Q38.
A. [ ]	A. [ ]	A. [ ]	A. [ ]	A. [ ]
B. [ ]	B. [ ]	B. [ ]	B. [ ]	B. [ ]
C. [ ]	C. [ ]	C. [ ]	C. [ ]	C. [ ]
D. [ ]	D. [ ]	D. [ ]	D. [ ]	D. [ ]
X. [ ]	X. [ ]	X. [ ]	X. [ ]	X. [ ]

Q39.	Q40.	Q41.	Q42.	Q43.
A. [ ]	A. [ ]	A. [ ]	A. [ ]	A. [ ]
B. [ ]	B. [ ]	B. [ ]	B. [ ]	B. [ ]
C. [ ]	C. [ ]	C. [ ]	C. [ ]	C. [ ]
D. [ ]	D. [ ]	D. [ ]	D. [ ]	D. [ ]
X. [ ]	X. [ ]	X. [ ]	X. [ ]	X. [ ]

Q44.	Q45.	Q46.	Q47.	Q48.
A. [ ]	A. [ ]	A. [ ]	A. [ ]	A. [ ]
B. [ ]	B. [ ]	B. [ ]	B. [ ]	B. [ ]
C. [ ]	C. [ ]	C. [ ]	C. [ ]	C. [ ]
D. [ ]	D. [ ]	D. [ ]	D. [ ]	D. [ ]
E. [ ]	E. [ ]	E. [ ]	E. [ ]	E. [ ]

Q49.	Q50.
A. [ ]	A. [ ]
B. [ ]	B. [ ]
C. [ ]	C. [ ]
D. [ ]	D. [ ]
E. [ ]	E. [ ]

Tutor Master Services

ENGLISH
Composition/Essay

30 minutes
Total Marks: 50

Choose one of these to write

1. In the story you have read, a magic ring plays an important part in helping Aladdin and his family. Imagine what you could do, if you were to come into possession of a magic ring. Write a story describing your adventures. Remember, you will need to tell the reader how you came to possess the ring, how you discover its magical powers and how you use the ring. Use the title,

   "The Magic Ring"

OR

2. In the story you have read, Aladdin finds treasure hidden in an underground cave. We believe it to have been gold, silver, jewellery and precious stones. However, we often value or treasure things that belong to us and are important. They may or may not be worth lots of money. Write about some things that are precious, or like treasure to you. Explain what each item is and describe it carefully. Then tell why it is so important and valuable to you.

   You should aim to write about up to three things and try to include some speech conversation at some point. Use the title,

   "My Treasured Possessions"

- Remember that the examiners are looking to see if you have included speech correctly punctuated, feelings (of yourself or your characters) and good description.
- Remember to check your grammar, spelling and punctuation carefully.
- Write on lined paper.
- If you make a mistake, cross it out neatly and write in your correction.

www.tutormaster-services.co.uk www.tutormaster-services.co.uk www.tutormaster-services.co.uk www.tutormaster-services.co.uk

Tutor Master Services

ENGLISH
Comprehension
Multiple Choice Introductory
Paper 2B

50 minutes

Read the following carefully:

1. You should read the passage and then answer the questions about it. It is a good idea to look back at the passage to check your answers as many times as you want. There are also some spelling, punctuation and grammar exercises to do.
2. This is a multiple-choice test. You need to mark your answer to each question on the answer sheet. You should mark only one answer for each question.
3. Draw a line clearly through the rectangle next to your answer. If you make a mistake, rub it out as fully as you can and mark in your new answer.
4. Mark your answer in the column that has the same number as the test question.
5. Try to do as many questions as you can. If you cannot do a question, move on to the next one. If you are not sure of an answer, have your best guess at the one you think may be correct.
6. Work as quickly and as carefully as you can.
7. You will have 50 minutes to do the comprehension and 30 minutes for the composition.

Published by:

Tutor Master Services, 61 Ashness Gardens, Greenford, Middlesex UB6 0RW.

ISBN: 978-0-9555909-6-2

Read the passage below and answer the following questions carefully. It is a good idea to go back and check the passage to find your answers. Write your answers neatly on the answer sheet.

Androcles and the Lion

In Roman times, many hundreds of years of ago, lived a slave called Androcles. Desperate for his freedom, Androcles escaped from his master and fled to the forest...

With the hot sun beating down on his back, legs aching and heart pumping Androcles eventually reached the forest. He knew he would be safe here and hoped he would be able to survive if he were able to avoid wild animals and find enough roots and berries to eat. As a runaway slave he knew he would be executed if caught.

As Androcles peered around him, anxiously looking for pursuers, he felt the first splash of raindrops on his skin. It would soon be getting dark and he knew he needed to find shelter for the night. Through a gap in the trees Androcles spotted the opening of a cave in the hillside and he decided it would be an ideal place to spend the night.

Moving cautiously, lest a sound should alert those searching for him, Androcles made his way hesitantly towards the gaping mouth of the cave. When he reached the sanctuary of the opening he stepped inside and breathed a deep sigh of relief as he knew now he would be safe. He looked around, eyes searching in the gloom for a place to rest. Suddenly, as his sight became accustomed to the half-light he noticed the unmistakable outline of a great beast... a lion!

With his heart pounding with fear, Androcles prayed that the lion had already eaten and would not want to devour him where he stood. Androcles began to back out of the cave when suddenly the lion raised its great head and groaned and moaned, sorrowfully, or so Androcles thought.

Slowly, he retraced his steps and as he neared the lion it put out its paw. Androcles saw immediately that it was all swollen and bleeding. Androcles could see a huge thorn had embedded itself in the lion's paw and was causing all the pain. Speaking quietly and reassuringly to the suffering animal, Androcles gently pulled out the thorn and using some cloth torn from the hem of his tunic, cleaned and bound up the wound. The lion licked the hand of Androcles appreciatively and then shuddered, groaned, sighed and fell asleep. Exhausted after his ordeal, Androcles too fell into a deep sleep.

For the next few weeks, Androcles and the lion lived together in the large cave. The lion quickly recovered from its injury and was able to hunt, bringing Androcles fresh meat each day. Androcles regained his strength and soon was able to hunt and gather food, together with his new friend.

Whilst out collecting water on his own one day, Androcles was startled. "Stand still!" ordered a savage voice, "we know who you are and there's a big reward for runaway slaves, you're coming with us."

www.tutormaster-services.co.uk www.tutormaster-services.co.uk www.tutormaster-services.co.uk www.tutormaster-services.co.uk

Androcles was captured and he knew there was no escape. Without delay Androcles was taken back to the city where he thought sadly about his friend, the lion, knowing they would never meet again.

Androcles was brought before the Roman Emperor in court and there he was sentenced to death. Confined in a small stone cell beneath the great arena Androcles awaited his execution.

On the appointed day, Androcles was led out into the arena. Jeering crowds thronged the terraces roaring their approval as a great lion was loosed. The lion, hungry, as it had not been fed for several days, bounded towards the helpless man. Roaring ravenously, the lion prepared to devour its victim.

Androcles knew he was finished and prepared for the onslaught of the first slashing blow and searing pain.

However, the expected wait for slashing claws and tearing jaws did not come. Instead, Androcles felt the tongue of the lion as it washed his face and licked him like a friendly dog. The lion recognised Androcles as his friend from the forest and nuzzled him as the man who had so gently cared for him.

The crowd was instantly silenced, and the Emperor astonished by what he had witnessed. He summoned Androcles to him, who told him the whole story.

"This man is pardoned," announced the Emperor, "and is to be set free. such kindness and gratitude between fierce enemies should be highly regarded. This is the lion, a man's friend; this is the man a lion's doctor."

At this Androcles was set free and the lion let loose to return to his native forest.

Answer these questions carefully. It is a good idea to go back and check the passage to find your answers. You should choose the best answer and mark its letter on your answer sheet.

1. From the opening two paragraphs we know that Androcles has been
   a) sauntering along
   b) ambling casually
   c) rambling slowly
   d) running fast
   e) strolling gently
2. His destination was
   a) a copse
   b) a wood
   c) a forest
   d) the jungle
   e) a cave
3. The three most important things for Androcles were to
   a) find food, avoid wild animals, avoid capture
   b) avoid food, find wild animals, escape capture
   c) eat wild animals, find food, be captured
   d) capture wild animals, avoid capture, avoid food
   e) find wild animals, escape food, avoid capture
4. The first thing that reminded Androcles that he needed to find shelter was when
   a) he spotted his pursuers
   b) he noticed a hidden cave
   c) the sun was setting
   d) he saw a gap in the trees
   e) he felt the splash of raindrops on his skin
5. Androcles decided that the best place to spend the night would be
   a) up a tree in the forest
   b) in a hole in the hillside
   c) in a hole by the seaside
   d) in a gap in the trees
   e) in the roots of the trees
6. As Androcles approached the cave he was probably feeling quite
   a) brave
   b) fearless
   c) bold
   d) nervous
   e) plucky

www.tutormaster-services.co.uk www.tutormaster-services.co.uk www.tutormaster-services.co.uk www.tutormaster-services.co.uk

7. When he was first inside the cave Androcles felt
   a) worried
   b) scared
   c) grateful
   d) concerned
   e) perturbed

8. When he noticed the lion Androcles suddenly felt
   a) apprehensive
   b) contented
   c) radiant
   d) gratified
   e) joyous

9. The main thing Androcles hoped the lion would not want to do was
   a) lick him
   b) stroke him
   c) cuddle him
   d) play with him
   e) consume him

10. The sounds made by the lion made Androcles think it was
    a) miserable
    b) jubilant
    c) cheery
    d) thrilled
    e) exuberant

11. The lion was appreciative of Androcles because he had shown
    a) indifference
    b) cruelty
    c) compassion
    d) apathy
    e) disinterest

12. We know that the friendship between Androcles and the lion grew because
    a) Androcles changed the bandages everyday
    b) Androcles hunted and brought the lion fresh meat
    c) they hunted separately
    d) the lion brought Androcles fresh meat each day
    e) the lion quickly recovered from his injury

13. Androcles was captured mainly because
    a) runaway slaves could work very hard
    b) his master was missing his companionship
    c) runaway slaves had a small bounty on their heads
    d) a recaptured slave was worth a lot of money
    e) it was quite unusual for slaves to run away

14. Once captured Androcles knew that his chances of escape were
    a) pretty slim
    b) nonexistent
    c) virtually certain
    d) very likely
    e) slightly possible

15. Androcles was taken back to the city
    a) quite soon
    b) after a rest
    c) soon after
    d) some time later
    e) immediately

16. To make sure that the lion would finish off its victim, it was
    a) starved for some time
    b) given extra treats
    c) allowed to wander at will
    d) treated like the King of the jungle
    e) permitted to enjoy extra portions

17. On hearing that the lion had been set loose, Androcles knew that his death was
    a) likely
    b) possible
    c) probable
    d) improbable
    e) inevitable

18. Surprisingly, the lion treated Androcles
    a) scornfully
    b) repulsively
    c) affectionately
    d) beseechingly
    e) dismissively

The following questions are about the meaning of words as they are used in the passage.

19. Another word for 'pursuers' (line 8) could be
    a) enemies
    b) fierce animals
    c) providers
    d) chasers ✓
    e) soldiers

20. The word closest in meaning to the word 'gloom' (line 17) is
    a) room
    b) murkiness ✓
    c) cave
    d) sunlight
    e) gleam

21. In line 44, we are told that Androcles was 'confined'. This means he was
    a) free to come and go
    b) held captive ✓
    c) awaiting release
    d) comfortably accommodated
    e) booked into

22. The word closest in meaning to the word 'nuzzled' (line 55) is
    a) devoured
    b) tasted
    c) embraced ✓
    d) chewed
    e) treated

23. The word most similar to 'sanctuary' (line 15) is
    a) shrine
    b) temple
    c) cave
    d) oasis
    e) refuge ✓

These questions are about words and phrases as they are used in the passage.

24. The phrase, "moving cautiously" (line 13) suggests that Androcles was
    - a) in a hurry
    - b) treading carefully
    - c) unconcerned
    - d) carefree
    - e) relaxed

25. The words, 'quietly' and 'reassuringly' (line 27) are examples of
    - a) nouns
    - b) verbs
    - c) adjectives
    - d) adverbs
    - e) proverbs

26. The phrase "he retraced his steps" (line 24) tells us that Androcles
    - a) drew around his footprints
    - b) walked backwards
    - c) went back the way he'd come
    - d) measured his stride
    - e) pressed on regardless

27. The phrase "jeering crowds" (lines 46) tells us that the spectators were
    - a) cheering excitedly
    - b) anticipating hopefully
    - c) taunting derisively
    - d) booing downheartedly
    - e) whooping jovially

28. The word closest in meaning to the word 'witnessed' (line 58) is
    - a) observed
    - b) judged
    - c) courted
    - d) undetected
    - e) missed

Read the following passage. There are some <u>*spelling*</u> mistakes. On each numbered line there is either <u>*one*</u> mistake or <u>*no*</u> mistake. Find the group of words with the mistake in it and mark its letter on your answer sheet. *If there is no mistake, mark* X.

Changing the Books

29. It was | time to | return books | to the libary.
A | B | C | D | X

30. Jody and Meg | dicided that | it would | be best
A | B | C | D | X

31. to make | their visit | early on a | Saterday morning.
A | B | C | D | X

32. When they | reached the | entrance they | found it was
A | B | C | D | X

33. closed and | so they | had to wait | in the qeue.
A | B | C | D | X

34. Eventually they | were delited | when the | librarian came.
A | B | C | D | X

35. Exitedly they | returned their | books and | went to choose
A | B | C | D | X

36. some new ones. | They found | exactly what | they wanted.
A | B | C | D | X

Read the following passage. There are some mistakes in the use of *capital letters* and *punctuation*. On each numbered line there is either <u>*one*</u> mistake or <u>*no*</u> mistake. Find the group of words with the mistake in it and mark its letter on your answer sheet. *If there is no mistake, mark* X.

Bike Riding

37. For their | birthday's Rishi | and Surina | got new bikes.
A | B | C | D | X

38. "Lets go | for a bike | ride on | the hill," suggested
A | B | C | D | X

39. Surina. so they carefully got ready and wheeled

Surina.	so	they carefully	got ready	and wheeled	
A	B	C	D		X

40. their bikes out of the garage and onto the road.

their bikes	out of the	garage and	onto the road.	
A	B	C	D	X

41. "Be very careful" exclaimed mum anxiously as they pedalled

"Be very careful"	exclaimed mum	anxiously as	they pedalled	
A	B	C	D	X

42. off down their road. "Watch me go, called Surina

off down	their road.	"Watch me go,	called Surina	
A	B	C	D	X

43. as she disappeared quickly over the top of the Hill.

as she	disappeared quickly	over the top	of the Hill.	
A	B	C	D	X

In each question you have to choose the *best word* or *group of words* to complete this passage so that it makes sense and is written in correct English. You should choose one of the five answers and mark its letter on your answer sheet.

In the Garden

44. Christine

think	thinked	thank	thought	thort
A	B	C	D	E

45. that it ... be

would	could	was	should	wasn't
A	B	C	D	E

46. a good day to do

some	sum	same	somed	sume
A	B	C	D	E

47. gardening. It was bright and the sun ... .

shine	shined	shining	shinning	shone
A	B	C	D	E

48. She ... up

pick	picked	picking	packed	pack
A	B	C	D	E

49. her spade and ... the soil.

digged	digging	dugged	dig	dug
A	B	C	D	E

50. Then she ... her seeds.

plant	plants	planted	will plant	planting
A	B	C	D	E

Answer Sheet

Mark your answer in the box with a line as shown using a pencil.
If you need to correct use a rubber to rub out. Do not cross out any change or make any other mark in the boxes.

Example	
a.	[ ]
b.	[ ]
c.	[—]
d.	[ ]
e.	[ ]

Q1.		Q2.		Q3.		Q4.		Q5.	
a.	[ ]	a.	[ ]	a.	[ ]	a.	[ ]	a.	[ ]
b.	[ ]	b.	[ ]	b.	[ ]	b.	[ ]	b.	[ ]
c.	[ ]	c.	[ ]	c.	[ ]	c.	[ ]	c.	[ ]
d.	[ ]	d.	[ ]	d.	[ ]	d.	[ ]	d.	[ ]
e.	[ ]	e.	[ ]	e.	[ ]	e.	[ ]	e.	[ ]

Q6.		Q7.		Q8.		Q9.		Q10.	
a.	[ ]	a.	[ ]	a.	[ ]	a.	[ ]	a.	[ ]
b.	[ ]	b.	[ ]	b.	[ ]	b.	[ ]	b.	[ ]
c.	[ ]	c.	[ ]	c.	[ ]	c.	[ ]	c.	[ ]
d.	[ ]	d.	[ ]	d.	[ ]	d.	[ ]	d.	[ ]
e.	[ ]	e.	[ ]	e.	[ ]	e.	[ ]	e.	[ ]

Q11.		Q12.		Q13.		Q14.		Q15.	
a.	[ ]	a.	[ ]	a.	[ ]	a.	[ ]	a.	[ ]
b.	[ ]	b.	[ ]	b.	[ ]	b.	[ ]	b.	[ ]
c.	[ ]	c.	[ ]	c.	[ ]	c.	[ ]	c.	[ ]
d.	[ ]	d.	[ ]	d.	[ ]	d	[ ]	d.	[ ]
e.	[ ]	e.	[ ]	e.	[ ]	e.	[ ]	e.	[ ]

Q16.		Q17.		Q18.		Q19.		Q20.	
a.	[ ]	a.	[ ]	a.	[ ]	a.	[ ]	a.	[ ]
b.	[ ]	b.	[ ]	b.	[ ]	b.	[ ]	b.	[ ]
c.	[ ]	c.	[ ]	c.	[ ]	c.	[ ]	c.	[ ]
d.	[ ]	d.	[ ]	d.	[ ]	d.	[ ]	d.	[ ]
e.	[ ]	e.	[ ]	e.	[ ]	e.	[ ]	e.	[ ]

Q21.		Q22.		Q23.		Q24.		Q25.	
a.	[ ]	a.	[ ]	a.	[ ]	a.	[ ]	a.	[ ]
b.	[ ]	b.	[ ]	b.	[ ]	b.	[ ]	b.	[ ]
c.	[ ]	c.	[ ]	c.	[ ]	c.	[ ]	c.	[ ]
d.	[ ]	d.	[ ]	d.	[ ]	d.	[ ]	d.	[ ]
e.	[ ]	e.	[ ]	e.	[ ]	e.	[ ]	e.	[ ]

Q26.		Q27.		Q28.	
a.	[ ]	a.	[ ]	a.	[ ]
b.	[ ]	b.	[ ]	b.	[ ]
c.	[ ]	c.	[ ]	c.	[ ]
d.	[ ]	d.	[ ]	d.	[ ]
e.	[ ]	e.	[ ]	e.	[ ]

Q29.	Q30.	Q31.	Q32.	Q33.
A. [ ]	A. [ ]	A. [ ]	A. [ ]	A. [ ]
B. [ ]	B. [ ]	B. [ ]	B. [ ]	B. [ ]
C. [ ]	C. [ ]	C. [ ]	C. [ ]	C. [ ]
D. [ ]	D. [ ]	D. [ ]	D. [ ]	D. [ ]
X. [ ]	X. [ ]	X. [ ]	X. [ ]	X. [ ]

Q34.	Q35.	Q36.	Q37.	Q38.
A. [ ]	A. [ ]	A. [ ]	A. [ ]	A. [ ]
B. [ ]	B. [ ]	B. [ ]	B. [ ]	B. [ ]
C. [ ]	C. [ ]	C. [ ]	C. [ ]	C. [ ]
D. [ ]	D. [ ]	D. [ ]	D. [ ]	D. [ ]
X. [ ]	X. [ ]	X. [ ]	X. [ ]	X. [ ]

Q39.	Q40.	Q41.	Q42.	Q43.
A. [ ]	A. [ ]	A. [ ]	A. [ ]	A. [ ]
B. [ ]	B. [ ]	B. [ ]	B. [ ]	B. [ ]
C. [ ]	C. [ ]	C. [ ]	C. [ ]	C. [ ]
D. [ ]	D. [ ]	D. [ ]	D. [ ]	D. [ ]
X. [ ]	X. [ ]	X. [ ]	X. [ ]	X. [ ]

Q44.	Q45.	Q46.	Q47.	Q48.
A. [ ]	A. [ ]	A. [ ]	A. [ ]	A. [ ]
B. [ ]	B. [ ]	B. [ ]	B. [ ]	B. [ ]
C. [ ]	C. [ ]	C. [ ]	C. [ ]	C. [ ]
D. [ ]	D. [ ]	D. [ ]	D. [ ]	D. [ ]
E. [ ]	E. [ ]	E. [ ]	E. [ ]	E. [ ]

Q49.	Q50.
A. [ ]	A. [ ]
B. [ ]	B. [ ]
C. [ ]	C. [ ]
D. [ ]	D. [ ]
E. [ ]	E. [ ]

Tutor Master Services

ENGLISH
Composition/Essay

30 minutes
Total Marks: 50

Choose one of these to write

1. In the story you have read, Androcles encounters a lion. Fortunately, the lion turns out to be friendly to him but as we know this story is a myth and in real life lions are best left well alone!

   However, it is possible to see wild animals at the zoo, Safari park, or even on a game reserve where people go on safari.

   Your task is to write imaginatively about a time when you encountered a wild animal or animals. Use the title,

   "**My Encounter with a Wild Animal**" or "**My Encounter with Wild Animals**"

OR

2. In the story you have read, we are told in lines 58 & 59 that Androcles was summoned by the Emperor to tell his story. Use your imagination to write out the speech conversation that takes place between them. Remember that the Emperor will have plenty of questions to ask Androcles, and Androcles will need to reply thoughtfully as he recalls his adventures.

   You should aim to write at least 20 lines. Use the title,

   "**Speech Conversation between Androcles and the Emperor**"

Remember that the examiners are looking to see if you have included speech correctly punctuated, feelings (of yourself or your characters) and good description.

- Remember to check your grammar, spelling and punctuation carefully.
- Write on lined paper.
- If you make a mistake, cross it out neatly and write in your correction.

www.tutormaster-services.co.uk www.tutormaster-services.co.uk www.tutormaster-services.co.uk www.tutormaster-services.co.uk

Tutor Master Services

ENGLISH
Comprehension
Multiple Choice Introductory
Paper 2C

50 minutes

Read the following carefully:

1. You should read the passage and then answer the questions about it. It is a good idea to look back at the passage to check your answers as many times as you want. There are also some spelling, punctuation and grammar exercises to do.
2. This is a multiple-choice test. You need to mark your answer to each question on the answer sheet. You should mark only one answer for each question.
3. Draw a line clearly through the rectangle next to your answer. If you make a mistake, rub it out as fully as you can and mark in your new answer.
4. Mark your answer in the column that has the same number as the test question.
5. Try to do as many questions as you can. If you cannot do a question, move on to the next one. If you are not sure of an answer, have your best guess at the one you think may be correct.
6. Work as quickly and as carefully as you can.
7. You will have 50 minutes to do the comprehension and 30 minutes for the composition.

Published by:

Tutor Master Services, 61 Ashness Gardens, Greenford, Middlesex UB6 0RW.

ISBN: 978-0-9555909-6-2

Read the passage below and answer the following questions carefully. It is a good idea to go back and check the passage to find your answers. Write your answers neatly on the answer sheet.

The Myth of Daedalus and Icarus

The tale of Daedalus (Day-da-lus) and Icarus (Ick-ar-us) goes back thousands of years to the time of ancient Greece. It is a myth, a made up story which the ancient Greek writers are famous for.

In ancient Greece there once lived a man named Daedalus. He lived and worked in the great city of Athens where he gained fame and fortune as a skilled and talented architect, sculptor and inventor who produced many fine works. Working alongside Daedalus and learning his trade was his nephew and apprentice Talus who seemed destined to become as great a workman as his uncle.

One day Talus came to Daedalus and showed him an invention he had developed. He had made a saw after watching how the teeth of a snake had used its jaws to cut. Surprisingly Daedalus was immediately jealous of Talus and in a fit of anger threw him off a tall building to his death. For this crime Daedalus was punished by the King of Greece and he was sent away to the island of Crete to work for King Minos.

While living on Crete, Daedalus met and married a beautiful woman and together they had a son named Icarus.

Now King Minos of Crete had a big problem. Living on the island was a fearsome and terrible monster known as the Minatour which had the head of a bull and the body of a man. He decided to imprison the creature in the Labyrinth, a series of underground caves. To build the caves King Minos instructed Daedalus to design and construct them, which he did.

Then one day the King of Athens - Theseus - arrived in Crete determined to kill the dreaded Minotaur, but he faced the problem of trying to find, kill the monster and then escape from the Labyrinth. King Minos had a daughter named Ariadne and she was determined to help Theseus in his quest to kill the Minotaur. She went to Daedalus and asked him to reveal to her the mystery of the Labyrinth. Daedalus instructed her and then, because she was in love with Theseus, she went to him to advise him. Ariadne provided Theseus with a ball of string which he used to help guide himself back out of the caves once he had killed the Minotaur.

When King Minos found out what Daedalus had done he was so enraged that he imprisioned Daedalus in a tall tower, all alone with Icarus, his young son.

Now Daedalus and Icarus did not like being prisoners and were determined to escape. Daedalus watched the birds flying over the sea towards Greece and thought to himself, "How free they are, if they can fly away, why can't we?" Daedalus and Icarus decided to use their skills to make wings to be able to fly to freedom.

Working secretly they used wax and string to fasten feathers to reeds of varying lengths. They made the wings very large so that they could support the heavy weight of a person and they put straps on them so that they could be attached to their arms. The wings were curved to imitate the curves of the birds' wings.

When their wings were ready, Daedalus gave his son a strict warning for when he was flying: if he flew too near to the sea his wings may dampen, get wet and he may fall in and be drowned, but if he flew too high in the sky, the heat of the sun would melt the wax on his wings and he would fall. Icarus promised to be careful.

So they set off, flying for freedom. At first everything went well, but the young Icarus, overwhelmed by the thrill of flying, began to try to do tricks and stunts. His father, concerned for his safety, ordered him to behave but Icarus was exhilarated by the sense of freedom and having too much fun, so he ignored his father's warning. Higher and higher he rose; upwards, upwards and nearer the sun, when suddenly the heat from the bright sunlight melted the wax in his wings. Icarus kept flapping and flapping his wings until he had no feathers left and he was only flapping his bare arms. Down, down, down he fell into the sea where he drowned.

Daedalus looked down to see feathers floating in the water and realised what had happened. Daedalus escaped to the island of Sicily but only after he had buried his son on a tiny island which nowadays is called Icaria. The sea around this island into which Icarus had plunged is named the Icarian sea to this very day.

Answer these questions carefully. It is a good idea to go back and check the passage to find your answers. You should choose the best answer and mark its letter on your answer sheet.

1. The first sentence tells us that Daedalus lived in Greece
   a) in recent times
   b) long ago
   c) in modern times
   d) not long past
   e) currently

2. Daedalus was related to Talus as he was
   a) his sister's son
   b) his brother's son
   c) either his brother or sister's son
   d) his cousin
   e) his son-in-law

3. Daedalus threw Talus off a tall building to his death mainly because he was
   a) content
   b) proud
   c) trusting
   d) reliable
   e) envious

4. Daedalus was banished from Greece which meant he was
   a) admitted
   b) received
   c) enrolled
   d) expelled
   e) accepted

5. While living on the island of Crete, Daedalus married and had a son called
   a) Icarus
   b) Talus
   c) Minos
   d) Theseus
   e) Ariadne

6. King Minos instructed Daedalus to design and construct the Labyrinth because he knew Daedalus was a skilled
   a) bricklayer
   b) artisan
   c) architect
   d) apprentice
   e) artist

7. The Minatour was a creature that can best be described as
   a) kind and gentle
   b) cuddly and cute
   c) warm and friendly
   d) alarming and forbidding
   e) benevolent and generous

8. The purpose of the Labyrinth was to
   a) provide a safe haven from the Minatour
   b) give an escape route from the Minatour
   c) give tourists the chance to see the Minatour
   d) contain the Minatour
   e) to hide the Minatour

9. The <u>main</u> problem that Theseus faced in the Labyrinth was
   a) making his entrance
   b) finding the entrance
   c) finding his way in
   d) making his exit
   e) finding the King's daughter

10. Theseus had an ally in his quest to kill the Minatour who was
   a) the King of Athens
   b) King Minos
   c) Ariadne
   d) the King of Crete
   e) Daedalus

11. The response of King Minos to what Daedalus had done was to
   a) put Daedalus and Icarus in an underground cell
   b) imprison both Daedalus and Icarus in a tall tower
   c) imprison Daedalus in a tall tower
   d) imprison Icarus in a tall tower
   e) cast both Daedalus and Icarus into the deep blue sea

12. Not wanting to be imprisoned, Daedalus and Icarus decided to escape by
   a) flying away
   b) swimming away
   c) running away
   d) sailing away
   e) rowing away

www.tutormaster-services.co.uk www.tutormaster-services.co.uk www.tutormaster-services.co.uk www.tutormaster-services.co.uk

13. The materials that Daedalus and Icarus used to make their wings were
   a) wax, string, feathers and weeds
   b) string, sacks, reeds and feathers
   c) straps, string, wax and feathers
   d) lengths, wax, string and feathers
   e) feathers, reeds, wax and string

14. The design of the wings included making them
   a) varying lengths, heavyweight and large
   b) curved, heavyweight and large
   c) large, with straps and curved
   d) supportive, attached and heavyweight
   e) strapped, curved and heavyweight

15. When it was time to escape Daedalus instructed Icarus to fly
   a) near the sun
   b) near the sea
   c) high
   d) low
   e) between the sea and the sun

16. Icarus began to do tricks and stunts as he flew because he felt
   a) excited
   b) bored
   c) frustrated
   d) listless
   e) uninspired

17. It is unlikely that Icarus would have plunged into the sea if he had been more
   a) rebellious
   b) defiant
   c) wilful
   d) wayward
   e) obedient

18. When Daedalus looked down and saw only feathers floating in the water, his feelings were mainly
   a) melancholy and mournful
   b) gratified and gleeful
   c) exhilarated and ecstatic
   d) elated and euphoric
   e) jubilant and joyous

www.tutormaster-services.co.uk www.tutormaster-services.co.uk www.tutormaster-services.co.uk www.tutormaster-services.co.uk

The following questions are about the meaning of words as they are used in the passage.

19. Another word for ‘destined’ (line 8) could be
    a) unlikely
    b) possibly
    c) perhaps
    d) certain
    e) maybe

20. The word closest in meaning to ‘jealous’ (line 12) could be
    a) proud
    b) resentful
    c) respectful
    d) gratified
    e) satisfied

21. The best meaning for the word for ‘imprison’ (line 20) is
    a) liberate
    b) loose
    c) free
    d) release
    e) detain

22. Another word for ‘dreaded’ (line 24) could be
    a) fearful
    b) cheerful
    c) genial
    d) agreeable
    e) merry

23. The word ‘Athens’ (line 5) is an example of
    a) an adjective
    b) a pronoun
    c) a proper noun
    d) a common noun
    e) an abstract noun

These questions are about words and phrases as they are used in the passage.

24. Daedalus "gained fame and fortune" (line 5). This means he became
    a) impoverished and infamous
    b) rich and famous
    c) penniless and anonymous
    d) unsung and destitute
    e) undistinguished and penniless

25. Ariadne "was determined to help Theseus in his quest" (line 26). This means she would
    a) desist from helping him in his search
    b) resist him in his search
    c) assist him in his search
    d) seek him in his search
    e) pursue him in his search

26. Ariadne went to Daedalus and "asked him to reveal to her the mystery of the Labyrinth" (line 27-28). This means she wanted him to
    a) conceal the puzzle of the Labyrinth
    b) hide the secret of the Labyrinth
    c) mask the enigma of the Labyrinth
    d) cloud the riddle of the Labyrinth
    e) disclose the secret of the Labyrinth

27. The phrase "to imitate the curves of the bird's wings" (lines 43 & 44) means to
    a) copy the shape of the bird's wings
    b) irritate the shape of the bird's wings
    c) contemplate the shape of the bird's wings
    d) to ignore the shape of the bird's wings
    e) to disregard the shape of the bird's wings

28. The phrase "exhilarated by the sense of freedom" (line 53) means Icarus was
    a) depressed to be free
    b) bored to be free
    c) distressed to be free
    d) excited to be free
    e) disheartened to be free

Read the following passage. There are some *spelling* mistakes. On each numbered line there is either *one* mistake or *no* mistake. Find the group of words with the mistake in it and mark its letter on your answer sheet. *If there is no mistake, mark* X.

The Outing

29. It was a | bright day | and the sun | was shinning.

A B C D X

30. Don felt it | was a good | day for a | faimly excursion.

A B C D X

31. His wife Gill | made some | tastey cakes, | pies and

A B C D X

32. sandwhiches that | they could | enjoy at | their leisure.

A B C D X

33. It was considered | that a | picknic would | be best

A B C D X

34. so they packed | a large hamper | full of snacks | and drinks.

A B C D X

35. Gill was driveing | and soon | they reached | their destination.

A B C D X

36. They settled | down to eat | delicious pies | and choclate cake.

A B C D X

Read the following passage. There are some mistakes in the use of *capital letters* and *punctuation*. On each numbered line there is either *one* mistake or *no* mistake. Find the group of words with the mistake in it and mark its letter on your answer sheet. *If there is no mistake, mark* X.

The Old Pot

37. One day | Doris was | digging her | beautiful garden.

A B C D X

38. As she dug | she suddenly | came across | an old pot.

A B C D X

39. She said to herself "This pot is nasty and dirty,"

A	B	C	D	X

40. so she threw the pot over the fence into Olives garden.

A	B	C	D	X

41. When olive was out in her garden one day

A	B	C	D	X

42. she found the dirty messy, old pot and picked

A	B	C	D	X

43. it up. when it was cleaned up it was very valuable.

A	B	C	D	X

In each question you have to choose the *best word* or *group of words* to complete this passage so that it makes sense and is written in correct English. You should choose one of the five answers and mark its letter on your answer sheet.

Firework Night

44. Ryan [knew | know | knows | new | knowing] that

A	B	C	D	E
knew	know	knows	new	knowing

45. November 5th [is | was | were | would | wouldn't] Firework Night.

A	B	C	D	E
is	was	were	would	wouldn't

46. His dad will [buyed | brought | buy | buys | bought] a good selection

A	B	C	D	E
buyed	brought	buy	buys	bought

47. of fireworks to [left | letted | letting | let | leave] off.

A	B	C	D	E
left	letted	letting	let	leave

48. Explosions of colour will [fill | filled | full | fulled | filling]

A	B	C	D	E
fill	filled	full	fulled	filling

49. the night sky [make | makeing | made | making | maked]

A	B	C	D	E
make	makeing	made	making	maked

50. it [enjoyable | enjoy | enjoying | enjoyed | enjoyd] for everyone.

A	B	C	D	E
enjoyable	enjoy	enjoying	enjoyed	enjoyd

Answer Sheet

Mark your answer in the box with a line as shown using a pencil.
If you need to correct use a rubber to rub out. Do not cross out any change or make any other mark in the boxes.

Example	
a.	[ ]
b.	[ ]
c.	[—]
d.	[ ]
e.	[ ]

	Q1.	Q2.	Q3.	Q4.	Q5.
a.	[ ]	[ ]	[ ]	[ ]	[ ]
b.	[ ]	[ ]	[ ]	[ ]	[ ]
c.	[ ]	[ ]	[ ]	[ ]	[ ]
d.	[ ]	[ ]	[ ]	[ ]	[ ]
e.	[ ]	[ ]	[ ]	[ ]	[ ]

	Q6.	Q7.	Q8.	Q9.	Q10.
a.	[ ]	[ ]	[ ]	[ ]	[ ]
b.	[ ]	[ ]	[ ]	[ ]	[ ]
c.	[ ]	[ ]	[ ]	[ ]	[ ]
d.	[ ]	[ ]	[ ]	[ ]	[ ]
e.	[ ]	[ ]	[ ]	[ ]	[ ]

	Q11.	Q12.	Q13.	Q14.	Q15.
a.	[ ]	[ ]	[ ]	[ ]	[ ]
b.	[ ]	[ ]	[ ]	[ ]	[ ]
c.	[ ]	[ ]	[ ]	[ ]	[ ]
d.	[ ]	[ ]	[ ]	[ ]	[ ]
e.	[ ]	[ ]	[ ]	[ ]	[ ]

	Q16.	Q17.	Q18.	Q19.	Q20.
a.	[ ]	[ ]	[ ]	[ ]	[ ]
b.	[ ]	[ ]	[ ]	[ ]	[ ]
c.	[ ]	[ ]	[ ]	[ ]	[ ]
d.	[ ]	[ ]	[ ]	[ ]	[ ]
e.	[ ]	[ ]	[ ]	[ ]	[ ]

	Q21.	Q22.	Q23.	Q24.	Q25.
a.	[ ]	[ ]	[ ]	[ ]	[ ]
b.	[ ]	[ ]	[ ]	[ ]	[ ]
c.	[ ]	[ ]	[ ]	[ ]	[ ]
d.	[ ]	[ ]	[ ]	[ ]	[ ]
e.	[ ]	[ ]	[ ]	[ ]	[ ]

	Q26.	Q27.	Q28.
a.	[ ]	[ ]	[ ]
b.	[ ]	[ ]	[ ]
c.	[ ]	[ ]	[ ]
d.	[ ]	[ ]	[ ]
e.	[ ]	[ ]	[ ]

Q29.
A. [ ]
B. [ ]
C. [ ]
D. [ ]
X. [ ]

Q30.
A. [ ]
B. [ ]
C. [ ]
D. [ ]
X. [ ]

Q31.
A. [ ]
B. [ ]
C. [ ]
D. [ ]
X. [ ]

Q32.
A. [ ]
B. [ ]
C. [ ]
D. [ ]
X. [ ]

Q33.
A. [ ]
B. [ ]
C. [ ]
D. [ ]
X. [ ]

Q34.
A. [ ]
B. [ ]
C. [ ]
D. [ ]
X. [ ]

Q35.
A. [ ]
B. [ ]
C. [ ]
D. [ ]
X. [ ]

Q36.
A. [ ]
B. [ ]
C. [ ]
D. [ ]
X. [ ]

Q37.
A. [ ]
B. [ ]
C. [ ]
D. [ ]
X. [ ]

Q38.
A. [ ]
B. [ ]
C. [ ]
D. [ ]
X. [ ]

Q39.
A. [ ]
B. [ ]
C. [ ]
D. [ ]
X. [ ]

Q40.
A. [ ]
B. [ ]
C. [ ]
D. [ ]
X. [ ]

Q41.
A. [ ]
B. [ ]
C. [ ]
D. [ ]
X. [ ]

Q42.
A. [ ]
B. [ ]
C. [ ]
D. [ ]
X. [ ]

Q43.
A. [ ]
B. [ ]
C. [ ]
D. [ ]
X. [ ]

Q44.
A. [ ]
B. [ ]
C. [ ]
D. [ ]
E. [ ]

Q45.
A. [ ]
B. [ ]
C. [ ]
D. [ ]
E. [ ]

Q46.
A. [ ]
B. [ ]
C. [ ]
D. [ ]
E. [ ]

Q47.
A. [ ]
B. [ ]
C. [ ]
D. [ ]
E. [ ]

Q48.
A. [ ]
B. [ ]
C. [ ]
D. [ ]
E. [ ]

Q49.
A. [ ]
B. [ ]
C. [ ]
D. [ ]
E. [ ]

Q50.
A. [ ]
B. [ ]
C. [ ]
D. [ ]
E. [ ]

Tutor Master Services

ENGLISH
Composition/Essay

30 minutes
Total Marks: 50

Choose one of these to write

1. In the story you have read, Theseus had to find his way into the Labyrinth - a series of underground caves - kill the Minatour and escape. Without the help of Ariadne he would have become lost and never found his way out.

   Your task is to write a story based upon a time when you felt you were lost. This may have been because you or the people you were with, could not find your way somewhere, or it could be about a time when you lost some people you were supposed to be with, e.g. your parents, relations or friends.

   Use the title, "**Lost**"

   OR

2. In the story you have read, Daedalus and Icarus escape from Crete by flying to freedom. However their story does not end well when Icarus crashes into the sea. Fortunately, flights do not usually end like this!

   Your task is write about an aspect of flight that you are familiar with. It could be about a time you flew in an aeroplane, when you made and flew a model aeroplane, or even perhaps if you knew something about birds and how they fly.

   Use your imagination and experiences to write a story using the title, "**Flight**"

Tutor Master Services

ENGLISH Comprehension

Multiple Choice Introductory Paper 2D

50 minutes

Read the following carefully:

1. You should read the passage and then answer the questions about it. It is a good idea to look back at the passage to check your answers as many times as you want. There are also some spelling, punctuation and grammar exercises to do.
2. This is a multiple-choice test. You need to mark your answer to each question on the answer sheet. You should mark only one answer for each question.
3. Draw a line clearly through the rectangle next to your answer. If you make a mistake, rub it out as fully as you can and mark in your new answer.
4. Mark your answer in the column that has the same number as the test question.
5. Try to do as many questions as you can. If you cannot do a question, move on to the next one. If you are not sure of an answer, have your best guess at the one you think may be correct.
6. Work as quickly and as carefully as you can.
7. You will have 50 minutes to do the comprehension and 30 minutes for the composition.

Published by:

Tutor Master Services, 61 Ashness Gardens, Greenford, Middlesex UB6 0RW.

ISBN: 978-0-9555909-6-2

Read the passage below and answer the following questions carefully. It is a good idea to go back and check the passage to find your answers. Write your answers neatly on the answer sheet.

The Wild Wood

In this extract from 'The Wind in the Willows', Mr Mole decides to pay a visit to Mr Badger who lives deep in the Wild Wood.

It was a cold still afternoon when Mr Mole slipped out of his warm snug parlour to visit Mr Badger in the Wild Wood. Now that the leafy summer was over, the countryside lay undecorated, hard and stripped of its finery. With great cheerfulness of spirit, Mole pushed on towards the Wild Wood which lay before him low and threatening like a black reef in some still southern sea.

There was nothing to alarm him at first. Twigs crackled under his feet, logs tripped him up, trees took on ugly crouching shapes that seemed to approach him on every side.

Everything was very still now. The light was fading as dusk advanced on him steadily, rapidly, gathering in behind and before; the light seemed to be draining away like flood-water. Mole began to feel frightened.

Then the faces began.

It was over his shoulder and indistinctly that he first thought he saw a face: a little wedge-shaped face, looking out at him from a hole. When he turned and confronted it, the thing had vanished.

He quickened his pace, telling himself cheerfully not to begin imagining things, or there would simply be no end of it. He passed another hole, and another, and another, and then - yes! - no! - yes! Certainly a little narrow face, with hard eyes, had flashed up for an instant from a hole and was gone. Mole hesitated - braced himself up for an effort and strode on. Then suddenly, every hole, far and near, and there were hundreds of them, seemed to possess its face, coming and going rapidly, all fixing on him glances of malice and hatred: all hard-eyed and evil and sharp.

If only he could get away from the holes in the banks, he thought, there would be no more faces. He swung off the path and plunged into the untrodden places of the wood.

Then the whistling began.

Very faint and shrill it was, and far behind him, when first he heard it; but somehow it made him hurry forward. Then, still very faint and shrill it sounded far ahead of him and made him hesitate and want to go back. As he halted in indecision it broke out on either side. They were up and alert and ready, evidently, whoever they were! And he - he was alone, and unarmed, and far from any help and the night was closing in.

Then the pattering began.

He thought it was only falling leaves at first, so slight and delicate was the sound of it. Then as the sound grew it took a regular rhythm and he knew it for nothing else but the pat-pat-pat of tiny feet, still a long way off. Was it in front or behind? It seemed to be first one, then the other, then both. It grew and it multiplied, till from every quarter as he listened anxiously, leaning this way and that, it seemed to be closing in on him. As he stood still to hearken, a rabbit came running hard towards him through the trees. He waited, expecting it to slacken pace, or to swerve from him into a different course. Instead the animal almost brushed him as it dashed past, his face set and hard, his eyes staring. "Get out of this, you fool, get out!" Mr Mole heard him mutter as he swung round a tree stump and disappeared down a friendly burrow.

Meanwhile, Rat had discovered Mole was not at home. He saw his footprints outside leading to the Wild Wood. Seizing a stout stick, he set out at a smart pace to track him. At last he found Mr Mole huddled in the shelter of an old beech tree, trembling all over and so glad his friend had come.

From *The Wind in the Willows* by Kenneth Grahame

Answer these questions carefully. It is a good idea to go back and check the passage to find your answers. You should choose the best answer and mark its letter on your answer sheet.

1. On the day that Mr Mole went visiting, the weather was
   a) warm and sunny
   b) bright and windy
   c) chilly and windless
   d) sunny and windy
   e) warm and windy

2. The time of year when he went visiting was probably
   a) early summer
   b) mid summer
   c) mid winter
   d) late spring
   e) late autumn

3. On the afternoon that Mole went visiting his mood can be best described as
   a) sad
   b) dejected
   c) glum
   d) merry
   e) forlorn

4. Not long after setting out on his walk Mole began to feel
   a) cheerful
   b) alarmed
   c) jolly
   d) brave
   e) jubilant

5. Mole began to feel apprehensive mainly because it was getting
   a) too warm
   b) too cold
   c) too murky
   d) too sunny
   e) pitch black

6. What really caused Mole to become frightened was when he started seeing
   a) weird faces
   b) holes in the bank
   c) flood water
   d) scary looking trees
   e) big logs

7. Mole's response to what he was seeing was to
   a) turn and run like mad
   b) slow down
   c) walk more carefully
   d) believe he was imagining it
   e) end his walk

8. In order to escape from what he was seeing, Mole decided to
   a) look straight ahead
   b) swing from tree branches
   c) plunge into the flood waters
   d) cover up the holes
   e) change direction

9. Next Mole heard whistling that was
   a) piercing and weak
   b) loud and piercing
   c) deep and low
   d) loud and clear
   e) loud and low

10. When Mole heard the whistling his reaction was to
   a) turn and run
   b) join in the whistling
   c) press on hastily
   d) give up and go home
   e) retrace his steps

11. When Mole heard the whistling ahead of him his reaction was to
   a) turn and head for home
   b) carry on regardless
   c) feel confident and reassured
   d) be unsure whether or not to continue
   e) shout for help

12. Mole concluded he was in danger because
   a) he was alone, had no arms, had help, was near safety
   b) he was alone, night was falling, he had no help nor weapons
   c) help was at hand, badger came by, he had a gun, moonlight helped
   d) he saw faces whistling, the sun came up, his arms were strong, he felt fearless
   e) he was alone, had no weapons, help was at hand, darkness fell

13. At first, Mole thought that the pattering sound was caused by
    a) leaves rustling
    b) raindrops falling
    c) leaves dropping
    d) twigs crackling
    e) branches brushing

14. The sound of the tiny feet can best be described as
    a) erratic motion
    b) occasional rhyme
    c) unsteady steps
    d) irregular rhythm
    e) constant tempo

15. As he stood listening Mole was feeling
    a) carefree
    b) worried
    c) unconcerned
    d) untroubled
    e) unworried

16. When Mole saw the rabbit coming towards him, he expected it to do one of two things
    a) slow down or change direction
    b) alter course or speed up
    c) alter course or change direction
    d) hasten or maintain direction
    e) slow down and chat to him

17. The rabbit issued Mole with
    a) a friendly greeting
    b) a cheerful acknowledgement
    c) the best of wishes
    d) a stark warning
    e) a warm welcome

18. When Rat discovered Mole he
    a) was huddled in the shelter of an old beech tree
    b) had stopped for a drink at the Old Beech Tree
    c) was very scared, frightened and trembling
    d) was not lost in the Wild Wood
    e) was not at home

The following questions are about the meaning of words as they are used in the passage.

19. Another word for 'alarm' (line 9) could be
    a) cheer
    b) frighten
    c) signal
    d) warn
    e) siren

20. The word closest in meaning to 'dusk' (line 12) is
    a) twilight
    b) sunrise
    c) dawn
    d) sun up
    e) noon day

21. The word 'indecision' (line 34) tells us that Mole was
    a) confident
    b) decisive
    c) resolved
    d) undecided
    e) determined

22. The word most similar to 'hearken' (line 44) is
    a) wait
    b) pause
    c) listen
    d) linger
    e) loiter

These questions are about words and phrases as they are used in the passage.

23. The phrase "like a black reef in some still southern sea" (line 7 & 8) is an example of
    a) alliteration
    b) personification
    c) metaphor
    d) simile
    e) persuasion

24. The phrase "dusk advanced" (line 12) tell us it was
    a) noon
    b) lunch time
    c) evening
    d) dawn
    e) sunrise

25. The words 'little' (line 21), 'narrow' and 'hard' (line 22) are examples of
    a) prepositions
    b) pronouns
    c) verbs
    d) adverbs
    e) adjectives

26. The phrase "till from every quarter" (lines 42) suggests that the sound was coming
    a) every fraction of a second
    b) fractionally one sound after another
    c) from one corner, then another
    d) from all around
    e) multiplying a quarter by a quarter

27. The phrase "friendly burrow" (lines 49) most accurately tells us this was
    a) a place of safety
    b) a place friendly for rabbits
    c) where the rabbit's friend lives
    d) a place his friend said he could borrow
    e) a place to avoid at all costs

28. The phrase "seizing a stout stick" (line 51) is an example of
    a) personification
    b) alliteration
    c) ellipsis
    d) comprehension
    e) complication

www.tutormaster-services.co.uk www.tutormaster-services.co.uk www.tutormaster-services.co.uk www.tutormaster-services.co.uk

Read the following passage. There are some *spelling* mistakes. On each numbered line there is either *one* mistake or *no* mistake. Find the group of words with the mistake in it and mark its letter on your answer sheet. *If there is no mistake, mark* X.

Washing the Car

29. Ruth and Dan | thourght that | they should | wash their

A B C D X

30. car. They | found the | bucket and | spunge which

A B C D X

31. were required | and the | special bottle | of liqwid.

A B C D X

32. Dan quickley | filled the | bucket to | the brim

A B C D X

33. then went | to turn | off the | tap before

A B C D X

34. it overflowed. | On the way | he stoped | to speak

A B C D X

35. too one | of their | children. When | he returned

A B C D X

36. he found | the pale | had overflowed | onto the floor.

A B C D X

Read the following passage. There are some mistakes in the use of *capital letters* and *punctuation*. On each numbered line there is either *one* mistake or *no* mistake. Find the group of words with the mistake in it and mark its letter on your answer sheet. *If there is no mistake, mark* X.

After Work

37. Mr Patel came | home from work | after a | busy day

A B C D X

38. his wife | made him | a nice cup | of hot tea.

A B C D X

39. “Thank you very much” he said, “that’s great.”

“Thank you	very much”	he said,	“that’s great.”	
A	B	C	D	X

40. “Your’e welcome,” she replied, “I thought you’d need it.”

“Your’e welcome,”	she replied,	“I thought	you’d need it.”	
A	B	C	D	X

41. Later on they sat down and watched “eastenders” on television

Later on	they sat down	and watched	“eastenders” on television	
A	B	C	D	X

42. After watching television, they went into the garden

After watching	television, they	went into	the garden	
A	B	C	D	X

43. and watered the plants cut the grass and picked flowers.

and watered the	plants cut the	grass and	picked flowers.	
A	B	C	D	X

In each question you have to choose the *best word* or *group of words* to complete this passage so that it makes sense and is written in correct English. You should choose one of the five answers and mark its letter on your answer sheet.

On the Underground

44. Anika and Rishil

wants	want	wanted	will want	whanted
A	B	C	D	E

45. to go shopping in London. They

travel	traveled	travelled	travell	travelling
A	B	C	D	E

46. by train. The doors were ... so they

opening	opened	closed	open	closing
A	B	C	D	E

47. had to ... on

jumping	jumped	jump	would jump	exit
A	B	C	D	E

48. ... before

quick	quickly	quicker	quickest	qwickly
A	B	C	D	E

49. the train ... the platform.

arrived	returned	resumed	left	stopped
A	B	C	D	E

50. They were just ... time.

at	out	late	right	in
A	B	C	D	E

Answer Sheet

Mark your answer in the box with a line as shown using a pencil.
If you need to correct use a rubber to rub out. Do not cross out any change or make any other mark in the boxes.

Example	
a.	[ ]
b.	[ ]
c.	[—]
d.	[ ]
e.	[ ]

Q1.	Q2.	Q3.	Q4.	Q5.
a. [ ]	a. [ ]	a. [ ]	a. [ ]	a. [ ]
b. [ ]	b. [ ]	b. [ ]	b. [ ]	b. [ ]
c. [ ]	c. [ ]	c. [ ]	c. [ ]	c. [ ]
d. [ ]	d. [ ]	d. [ ]	d. [ ]	d. [ ]
e. [ ]	e. [ ]	e. [ ]	e. [ ]	e. [ ]

Q6.	Q7.	Q8.	Q9.	Q10.
a. [ ]	a. [ ]	a. [ ]	a. [ ]	a. [ ]
b. [ ]	b. [ ]	b. [ ]	b. [ ]	b. [ ]
c. [ ]	c. [ ]	c. [ ]	c. [ ]	c. [ ]
d. [ ]	d. [ ]	d. [ ]	d. [ ]	d. [ ]
e. [ ]	e. [ ]	e. [ ]	e. [ ]	e. [ ]

Q11.	Q12.	Q13.	Q14.	Q15.
a. [ ]	a. [ ]	a. [ ]	a. [ ]	a. [ ]
b. [ ]	b. [ ]	b. [ ]	b. [ ]	b. [ ]
c. [ ]	c. [ ]	c. [ ]	c. [ ]	c. [ ]
d. [ ]	d. [ ]	d. [ ]	d. [ ]	d. [ ]
e. [ ]	e. [ ]	e. [ ]	e. [ ]	e. [ ]

Q16.	Q17.	Q18.	Q19.	Q20.
a. [ ]	a. [ ]	a. [ ]	a. [ ]	a. [ ]
b. [ ]	b. [ ]	b. [ ]	b. [ ]	b. [ ]
c. [ ]	c. [ ]	c. [ ]	c. [ ]	c. [ ]
d. [ ]	d. [ ]	d. [ ]	d. [ ]	d. [ ]
e. [ ]	e. [ ]	e. [ ]	e. [ ]	e. [ ]

Q21.	Q22.	Q23.	Q24.	Q25.
a. [ ]	a. [ ]	a. [ ]	a. [ ]	a. [ ]
b. [ ]	b. [ ]	b. [ ]	b. [ ]	b. [ ]
c. [ ]	c. [ ]	c. [ ]	c. [ ]	c. [ ]
d. [ ]	d. [ ]	d. [ ]	d. [ ]	d. [ ]
e. [ ]	e. [ ]	e. [ ]	e. [ ]	e. [ ]

Q26.	Q27.	Q28.
a. [ ]	a. [ ]	a. [ ]
b. [ ]	b. [ ]	b. [ ]
c. [ ]	c. [ ]	c. [ ]
d. [ ]	d. [ ]	d. [ ]
e. [ ]	e. [ ]	e. [ ]

www.tutormaster-services.co.uk www.tutormaster-services.co.uk www.tutormaster-services.co.uk www.tutormaster-services.co.uk

Q29.	Q30.	Q31.	Q32.	Q33.
A. [ ]	A. [ ]	A. [ ]	A. [ ]	A. [ ]
B. [ ]	B. [ ]	B. [ ]	B. [ ]	B. [ ]
C. [ ]	C. [ ]	C. [ ]	C. [ ]	C. [ ]
D. [ ]	D. [ ]	D. [ ]	D. [ ]	D. [ ]
X. [ ]	X. [ ]	X. [ ]	X. [ ]	X. [ ]

Q34.	Q35.	Q36.	Q37.	Q38.
A. [ ]	A. [ ]	A. [ ]	A. [ ]	A. [ ]
B. [ ]	B. [ ]	B. [ ]	B. [ ]	B. [ ]
C. [ ]	C. [ ]	C. [ ]	C. [ ]	C. [ ]
D. [ ]	D. [ ]	D. [ ]	D. [ ]	D. [ ]
X. [ ]	X. [ ]	X. [ ]	X. [ ]	X. [ ]

Q39.	Q40.	Q41.	Q42.	Q43.
A. [ ]	A. [ ]	A. [ ]	A. [ ]	A. [ ]
B. [ ]	B. [ ]	B. [ ]	B. [ ]	B. [ ]
C. [ ]	C. [ ]	C. [ ]	C. [ ]	C. [ ]
D. [ ]	D. [ ]	D. [ ]	D. [ ]	D. [ ]
X. [ ]	X. [ ]	X. [ ]	X. [ ]	X. [ ]

Q44.	Q45.	Q46.	Q47.	Q48.
A. [ ]	A. [ ]	A. [ ]	A. [ ]	A. [ ]
B. [ ]	B. [ ]	B. [ ]	B. [ ]	B. [ ]
C. [ ]	C. [ ]	C. [ ]	C. [ ]	C. [ ]
D. [ ]	D. [ ]	D. [ ]	D. [ ]	D. [ ]
E. [ ]	E. [ ]	E. [ ]	E. [ ]	E. [ ]

Q49.	Q50.
A. [ ]	A. [ ]
B. [ ]	B. [ ]
C. [ ]	C. [ ]
D. [ ]	D. [ ]
E. [ ]	E. [ ]

Tutor Master Services

ENGLISH
Composition/Essay

30 minutes
Total Marks: 50

Choose one of these to write

1. In the story you have read, Mole ventures into the Wild Wood, a place which he is unfamiliar with and which turns out to be very scary. He sees strange sights and hears odd noises. Mole responds to these sights and sounds by panicking and behaving in a way that tells us he was frightened.

   Your task is to write a story telling about a time that you found yourself in a place that was unfamiliar. You may not have been alone and it may have been a pleasant or a frightening place. Describe the place, what you saw and heard and how you felt. Describe carefully so that the reader can imagine what you were experiencing. Use the title,

   "**An Unfamiliar Place**"

OR

2. At the end of the story you have read, Rat finds Mole huddled in the shelter of an old tree. They are glad to have found each other. Use your imagination to write out the speech conversation that takes place between them. Remember that Rat will be anxious to find out what happened to Mole, and Mole will try to answer Rat's questions as he recounts the events.

   You should aim to write at least 20 lines. Use the title,

   "**Speech Conversation between Mole and Rat**"

- Remember that the examiners are looking to see if you have included speech correctly punctuated, feelings (of yourself or your characters) and good description.
- Remember to check your grammar, spelling and punctuation carefully.
- Write on lined paper.
- If you make a mistake, cross it out neatly and write in your correction.

www.tutormaster-services.co.uk www.tutormaster-services.co.uk www.tutormaster-services.co.uk www.tutormaster-services.co.uk

Tutor Master Services

ENGLISH
Comprehension
Multiple Choice Introductory
Paper 2E

50 minutes

Read the following carefully:

1. You should read the passage and then answer the questions about it. It is a good idea to look back at the passage to check your answers as many times as you want. There are also some spelling, punctuation and grammar exercises to do.
2. This is a multiple-choice test. You need to mark your answer to each question on the answer sheet. You should mark only one answer for each question.
3. Draw a line clearly through the rectangle next to your answer. If you make a mistake, rub it out as fully as you can and mark in your new answer.
4. Mark your answer in the column that has the same number as the test question.
5. Try to do as many questions as you can. If you cannot do a question, move on to the next one. If you are not sure of an answer, have your best guess at the one you think may be correct.
6. Work as quickly and as carefully as you can.
7. You will have 50 minutes to do the comprehension and 30 minutes for the composition.

Published by:

Tutor Master Services, 61 Ashness Gardens, Greenford, Middlesex UB6 0RW.

ISBN: 978-0-9555909-6-2

www.tutormaster-services.co.uk www.tutormaster-services.co.uk www.tutormaster-services.co.uk www.tutormaster-services.co.uk

Read the passage below and answer the following questions carefully. It is a good idea to go back and check the passage to find your answers. Write your answers neatly on the answer sheet.

The Fire

This extract is from the story of 'Black Beauty'. It tells of the life, many years ago, of a young male horse – a colt. In this story the narrator is the horse.

Later on in the evening, a traveller's horse was brought in by a second ostler, and whilst he was cleaning him a young man with a pipe in his mouth lounged into the stable to gossip.

"I say, Towler," said the ostler, "just run up the ladder into the loft and bring down some hay into this horse's rack, will you? Only first lay down your pipe."

"All right," said the other, and he went up through the trap door. I heard him step across the floor overhead and put down the hay. James came in to look at us the last thing, and the door was locked.

I cannot say how long I had slept, nor what time in the night it was, but I woke up feeling very uncomfortable, though I hardly knew why. I got up; the air seemed all thick and choking. I heard Ginger coughing, and one of the other horses moved about restlessly. It was quite dark, and I could see nothing; but the stable was full of smoke, and I hardly knew how to breathe.

The trap door had been left open, and I thought that was the place from which the smoke came. I listened and heard a soft, rushing sort of noise, and a low crackling and snapping. I did not know what it was, but there was something in the sound so strange that it made me tremble all over. The other horses were now all awake; some were pulling at their halters, others were stamping.

At last I heard steps outside, and the ostler who had put up the traveller's horse burst into the stable with a lantern, and began to untie the horses, and try to lead them out; but he seemed in such a hurry, and was so frightened himself, that he frightened me still more. The first horse would not go with him; he tried the second and third, but they too would not stir. He came to me next and tried to drag me out of the stall by force; of course that was no use. He tried us all by turns and then left the stable.

No doubt we were very foolish, but danger seemed to be all round; there was nobody whom we knew to trust in, and all was strange and uncertain. The fresh air that had come in through the open door made it easier to breathe, but the rushing sound overhead grew louder, and as I looked upward, through the bars of my empty rack, I saw a red light flickering on the wall. Then I heard a cry of 'Fire!' outside, and the old ostler came quietly and quickly in. He got one horse out, and went to another; but the flames were playing round the trap door, and the roaring overhead was dreadful.

The next thing I heard was James's voice, quiet and cheery, as it always was.

*ostler = someone employed in a stable to take car of the horses

"Come, my beauties, it is time for us to be off, so wake up and come along." I stood nearest the door, so he came to me first, patting me as he came in.

"Come, Beauty, on with your bridle, my boy, we'll soon be out of this smother." It was on in no time; then he took the scarf off his neck, and tied it lightly over my eyes, and, patting and coaxing, he led me out of the stable. Safe in the yard, he slipped the scarf off my eyes, and shouted, "Here somebody! Take this horse while I go back for the other."

A tall, broad man stepped forward and took me, and James darted back into the stable. I set up a shrill whinny as I saw him go. Ginger told me afterwards that whinny was the best thing I could have done for her, for had she not heard me outside, she would never have had courage to come out.

There was much confusion in the yard; the horses were being got out of other stables, and the carriages and gigs were being pulled out of houses and sheds, lest the flames should spread further. On the other side of the yard windows were thrown open, and people were shouting all sorts of things; but I kept my eye fixed on the stable door, where the smoke poured out thicker than ever, and I could see flashes of red light.

Presently, I heard above all the stir and din a loud, clear voice, which I knew was master's:-

"James Howard! James Howard! Are you there?" There was no answer, but I heard a crash of something falling in the stable, and the next moment I gave a loud, joyful neigh, for I saw James coming through the smoke, leading Ginger with him; she was coughing violently and he was not able to speak.

"My brave lad!" said master, laying his hand on his shoulder. "Are you hurt?"

James shook his head for he could not speak yet.

"Ay," said the big man who held me, "he is a brave lad, and no mistake."

"And now," said master, "when you have got your breath, James, we'll get out of this place as quickly as we can."

We were moving towards the entry when from the Market Place there came a sound of galloping feet and loud rumbling wheels.

"Tis the fire engine! The fire engine!" shouted two or three voices. "Stand back, make way!" And clattering and thundering over the stones two horses dashed into the yard with the heavy engine behind them. The firemen leaped to the ground; there was no need to ask where the fire was – it was torching up in a great blaze from the roof.

From *Black Beauty* by Anna Sewell

Answer these questions carefully. It is a good idea to go back and check the passage to find your answers. You should choose the best answer and mark its letter on your answer sheet.

1. In this story the narrator is the horse. This means he is
   a) the storyteller
   b) the audience
   c) the listener
   d) the congregation
   e) the spectator
2. The main character in this story is a horse called
   a) Towler
   b) Ginger
   c) James
   d) Black Beauty
   e) Black Bess
3. In the story the time of day was
   a) morning
   b) noon
   c) night
   d) dawn
   e) sunrise
4. In paragraph two (lines 3-5) Towler is smoking a lighted
   a) cigarette
   b) cigar
   c) shisha pipe
   d) pipe
   e) snuff
5. The ostler told Towler to stop smoking mainly because
   a) smoking is bad for you
   b) it was making the ostler cough
   c) they couldn't see the horses
   d) smoke was getting in their eyes
   e) it might cause a fire in the stable
6. The one thing that did not waken the horses was
   a) they were feeling uncomfortable
   b) the air was thick
   c) the air was choking
   d) it was smoky
   e) the bright morning sunlight

7. The smoke seemed to be coming from the
   a) front door
   b) trap door
   c) back door
   d) side door
   e) chimney

8. The horses were reluctant to leave the stable because they
   a) were frightened to move
   b) were warm by the fire
   c) would prefer to stay together
   d) were sleepy after a hard day
   e) were comfortable in the hay

9. In paragraph 8 (lines 30-37) the flickering red light is likely to be a
   a) night light
   b) fire light
   c) street light
   d) danger light
   e) fire engine light

10. The horses went with James because his presence
    a) alarmed them
    b) perturbed them
    c) reassured them
    d) agitated them
    e) distressed them

11. In paragraph 11 (lines 46-50), the noise that encouraged Ginger to go outside is best described as a
    a) high-pitched neigh
    b) low growl
    c) monotonous whine
    d) soft purr
    e) sharp whistle

12. The scene in the yard can best be described as one of
    a) tranquillity
    b) serenity
    c) calmness
    d) peacefulness
    e) panic

13. The horse kept his eye "fixed on the stable door" (line 55) because
    a) he wanted to see the fire coming out
    b) he wanted to see the fire being put out
    c) there was too much smoke billowing out
    d) he wanted to see James and Ginger coming out
    e) if you see too much smoke you pass out

14. The master's voice (lines 57-58) can best be described as
    a) coherent and audible
    b) faint and indistinct
    c) muffled and inaudible
    d) muted and soft
    e) quiet and stifled

15. Neither James nor Ginger could speak because
    a) of all the noise and uproar
    b) they had inhaled too much smoke
    c) the smoke was in their eyes
    d) neither had anything to say
    e) they were overwhelmed with a sense of relief

16. The "galloping feet and rumbling wheels" (line 71) preceded the arrival of the
    a) cavalry
    b) mounted police
    c) Royal Horse Artillery
    d) fire engine
    e) chariots of fire

17. The building that had caught fire was the
    a) farm
    b) roof
    c) stable
    d) market
    e) yard

18. The word that best describes the horses' escape from the blaze is
    a) evacuated
    b) ejected
    c) expelled
    d) evicted
    e) expropriated

The following questions are about the meaning of words as they are used in the passage.

19. The word closest in meaning to the word 'gossip' (line 5) is
    a) discourse
    b) praise
    c) encourage
    d) chatter
    e) rumour

20. The word closest in meaning to the word 'stir' (line 27) is
    a) retire
    b) stay
    c) remain
    d) budge
    e) wait

21. Another word for 'coaxing' (line 43) could be
    a) persuading
    b) dissuading
    c) discouraging
    d) deterring
    e) declining

22. The word closest in meaning to 'violently' (line 62) is
    a) gently
    b) vigorously
    c) weakly
    d) mildly
    e) placidly

23. The word closest in meaning to 'darted' (line 46) is
    a) dashed
    b) ambled
    c) strolled
    d) sauntered
    e) wandered

These questions are about words and phrases as they are used in the passage.

24. The phrase, "He tried us all by turns ..." (line 29) means
    a) He tried to turn the horses round one by one.
    b) He turned the horses round one by one.
    c) He tried to move the horses out one by one.
    d) One by one the horses turn around.
    e) All the horses turned around one by one.

25. The phrase, "playing round the trap door" (line 37) means the flames were
    a) playing happily
    b) darting menacingly
    c) blazing cheerfully
    d) gleaming beautifully
    e) flaring merrily

26. The word most similar to 'din' (line 57) is
    a) silence
    b) hush
    c) peace
    d) tranquillity
    e) racket

27. The closest meaning to the phrase "and no mistake" (line 67) is
    a) and that's a lie
    b) and that's untrue
    c) we're all mistaken
    d) and that's a fact
    e) so be mistaken

28. The words, 'James', 'Ginger', 'Market Place' and 'Towler' are all examples of
    a) adjectives
    b) common nouns
    c) proper nouns
    d) similes
    e) metaphors

Read the following passage. There are some *spelling* mistakes. On each numbered line there is either *one* mistake or *no* mistake. Find the group of words with the mistake in it and mark its letter on your answer sheet. *If there is no mistake, mark* X.

Exploring

29. Tom and Sarah descided to visit an old castle

A	B	C	D	X
Tom and Sarah	descided to	visit an	old castle	

30. wich was near to their aunt's new house.

A	B	C	D	X
wich was	near to	their aunt's	new house.	

31. They were very exicted because they could explore

A	B	C	D	X
They were	very exicted	because they	could explore	

32. However they were surprised and dissapointed as there

A	B	C	D	X
However they	were surprised	and dissapointed	as there	

33. was apparently no way to find the entrance.

A	B	C	D	X
was apparently	no way	to find	the entrance.	

34. Undeterred they found to their suprise a hole

A	B	C	D	X
Undeterred they	found to	their suprise	a hole	

35. in the wall surrounding the old building. They climed

A	B	C	D	X
in the wall	surrounding the	old building.	They climed	

36. in thorough the hole and were soon exploring.

A	B	C	D	X
in thorough	the hole	and were	soon exploring.	

Read the following passage. There are some mistakes in the use of *capital letters* and *punctuation*. On each numbered line there is either *one* mistake or *no* mistake. Find the group of words with the mistake in it and mark its letter on your answer sheet. *If there is no mistake, mark* X.

Lunch in the Park

37. It was a sunny day so mrs Green went to the park.

A	B	C	D	X
It was	a sunny day	so mrs Green	went to the park.	

38. She ate her lunch of grapes crisps and a bun.

A	B	C	D	X
She ate her	lunch of	grapes crisps	and a bun.	

www.tutormaster-services.co.uk www.tutormaster-services.co.uk www.tutormaster-services.co.uk www.tutormaster-services.co.uk

39. Her magazine | was full | of new | recipe idea's and

A	B	C	D	X

40. she decided | to cook | something nice | that evening

A	B	C	D	X

41. Inviting her | friend seemed | like a | good idea

A	B	C	D	X

42. so she | called her | on her | mobile phone

A	B	C	D	X

43. "Would you | like to come | round for tea," | she asked.

A	B	C	D	X

In each question you have to choose the *best word* or *group of words* to complete this passage so that it makes sense and is written in correct English. You should choose one of the five answers and mark its letter on your answer sheet.

A Meal at a Restaurant

44. Saturday night [isn't / wasn't / were / weren't / is] a

A	B	C	D	E
isn't	wasn't	were	weren't	is

45. good time to [joy / enjoy / enjoyed / enjoyable / enjoying]

A	B	C	D	E
joy	enjoy	enjoyed	enjoyable	enjoying

46. a meal at a restaurant [thort / thank / thinking / thought / thorought] Ross.

A	B	C	D	E
thort	thank	thinking	thought	thorought

47. He decided to [book / booked / booking / cancel / booker]

A	B	C	D	E
book	booked	booking	cancel	booker

48. a table for himself and [a / same / some / few / many] friend.

A	B	C	D	E
a	same	some	few	many

49. The [group / crowd / pair / trio / party] of them

A	B	C	D	E
group	crowd	pair	trio	party

50. [eat / eated / eating / eatable / ate] till they were full.

A	B	C	D	E
eat	eated	eating	eatable	ate

Answer Sheet

Mark your answer in the box with a line as shown using a pencil.
If you need to correct use a rubber to rub out. Do not cross out any change or make any other mark in the boxes.

Example
a. [ ]
b. [ ]
c. [—]
d. [ ]
e. [ ]

Q1.
a. [ ]
b. [ ]
c. [ ]
d. [ ]
e. [ ]

Q2.
a. [ ]
b. [ ]
c. [ ]
d. [ ]
e. [ ]

Q3.
a. [ ]
b. [ ]
c. [ ]
d. [ ]
e. [ ]

Q4.
a. [ ]
b. [ ]
c. [ ]
d. [ ]
e. [ ]

Q5.
a. [ ]
b. [ ]
c. [ ]
d. [ ]
e. [ ]

Q6.
a. [ ]
b. [ ]
c. [ ]
d. [ ]
e. [ ]

Q7.
a. [ ]
b. [ ]
c. [ ]
d. [ ]
e. [ ]

Q8.
a. [ ]
b. [ ]
c. [ ]
d. [ ]
e. [ ]

Q9.
a. [ ]
b. [ ]
c. [ ]
d. [ ]
e. [ ]

Q10.
a. [ ]
b. [ ]
c. [ ]
d. [ ]
e. [ ]

Q11.
a. [ ]
b. [ ]
c. [ ]
d. [ ]
e. [ ]

Q12.
a. [ ]
b. [ ]
c. [ ]
d. [ ]
e. [ ]

Q13.
a. [ ]
b. [ ]
c. [ ]
d. [ ]
e. [ ]

Q14.
a. [ ]
b. [ ]
c [ ]
d. [ ]
e. [ ]

Q15.
a. [ ]
b. [ ]
c. [ ]
d. [ ]
e. [ ]

Q16.
a. [ ]
b. [ ]
c. [ ]
d. [ ]
e. [ ]

Q17.
a. [ ]
b. [ ]
c. [ ]
d. [ ]
e. [ ]

Q18.
a. [ ]
b. [ ]
c. [ ]
d. [ ]
e. [ ]

Q19.
a. [ ]
b. [ ]
c. [ ]
d. [ ]
e. [ ]

Q20.
a. [ ]
b. [ ]
c. [ ]
d. [ ]
e. [ ]

Q21.
a. [ ]
b. [ ]
c. [ ]
d. [ ]
e. [ ]

Q22.
a. [ ]
b. [ ]
c. [ ]
d. [ ]
e. [ ]

Q23.
a. [ ]
b. [ ]
c. [ ]
d. [ ]
e. [ ]

Q24.
a. [ ]
b. [ ]
c. [ ]
d. [ ]
e. [ ]

Q25.
a. [ ]
b. [ ]
c. [ ]
d. [ ]
e. [ ]

Q26.
a. [ ]
b. [ ]
c. [ ]
d. [ ]
e. [ ]

Q27.
a. [ ]
b. [ ]
c. [ ]
d. [ ]
e. [ ]

Q28.
a. [ ]
b. [ ]
c. [ ]
d. [ ]
e. [ ]

Q29.	Q30.	Q31.	Q32.	Q33.
A. [ ]	A. [ ]	A. [ ]	A. [ ]	A. [ ]
B. [ ]	B. [ ]	B. [ ]	B. [ ]	B. [ ]
C. [ ]	C. [ ]	C. [ ]	C. [ ]	C. [ ]
D. [ ]	D. [ ]	D. [ ]	D. [ ]	D. [ ]
X. [ ]	X. [ ]	X. [ ]	X. [ ]	X. [ ]

Q34.	Q35.	Q36.	Q37.	Q38.
A. [ ]	A. [ ]	A. [ ]	A. [ ]	A. [ ]
B. [ ]	B. [ ]	B. [ ]	B. [ ]	B. [ ]
C. [ ]	C. [ ]	C. [ ]	C. [ ]	C. [ ]
D. [ ]	D. [ ]	D. [ ]	D. [ ]	D. [ ]
X. [ ]	X. [ ]	X. [ ]	X. [ ]	X. [ ]

Q39.	Q40.	Q41.	Q42.	Q43.
A. [ ]	A. [ ]	A. [ ]	A. [ ]	A. [ ]
B. [ ]	B. [ ]	B. [ ]	B. [ ]	B. [ ]
C. [ ]	C. [ ]	C. [ ]	C. [ ]	C. [ ]
D. [ ]	D. [ ]	D. [ ]	D. [ ]	D. [ ]
X. [ ]	X. [ ]	X. [ ]	X. [ ]	X. [ ]

Q44.	Q45.	Q46.	Q47.	Q48.
A. [ ]	A. [ ]	A. [ ]	A. [ ]	A. [ ]
B. [ ]	B. [ ]	B. [ ]	B. [ ]	B. [ ]
C. [ ]	C. [ ]	C. [ ]	C. [ ]	C. [ ]
D. [ ]	D. [ ]	D. [ ]	D. [ ]	D. [ ]
E. [ ]	E. [ ]	E. [ ]	E. [ ]	E. [ ]

Q49.	Q50.
A. [ ]	A. [ ]
B. [ ]	B. [ ]
C. [ ]	C. [ ]
D. [ ]	D. [ ]
E. [ ]	E. [ ]

Tutor Master Services

ENGLISH
Composition/Essay

30 minutes
Total Marks: 50

Choose one of these to write

1. In the comprehension passage you have read, the dangers caused by fire are plain to see. Sometimes fire can be bad and dangerous but it can also at times be helpful, for example, it can keep us warm or help us celebrate special days.

   Think about a time when you experienced a fire. You may have seen one, been involved in one or been celebrating one. Now write a story about what happened. Use the title,

   "My Fire Experience"

OR

2. Imagine you are a reporter for a local newspaper. The day after the fire your editor asks you to write a report of what happened that night and in particular to highlight the heroic role played by young James Howard. Use information from the passage, plus your imagination to tell the story. You should include:

   a) How the fire began and how it spread (there are clues in the first 3 paragraphs)

   b) An account of how the horses were saved and in particular what James Howard did to help.

   c) An interview with James Howard about his feelings about what has happened and his actions.

   Use the newspaper headline,

   "Brave James the Hero in Stable Fire Rescue"

Tutor Master Services

ENGLISH Comprehension

Answers and Marking Schemes for Multiple Choice Introductory Papers 1 – 5 and Compositions

Answers to Paper 2A

1. d
2. e
3. c
4. b
5. e
6. a
7. d
8. c
9. e
10. e
11. b
12. c
13. d
14. a
15. b
16. c
17. e
18. a
19. b
20. d
21. c
22. b
23. c
24. e
25. a
26. c
27. b
28. d
29. B (disaster)
30. B (finished)
31. C (leisure)
32. B (watch)
33. A (noise)
34. X
35. A (happened)
36. X
37. D (play. – full stop at end of sentence)
38. A ("I'd – open speech mark required)
39. A (let's–- apostrophe required)
40. B (out – full stop not needed)
41. C (they'd – apostrophe required)
42. X
43. C (she'd – apostrophe incorrectly placed)
44. C
45. C
46. A
47. D
48. B
49. E
50. D

Answers to Paper 2B

1. d
2. c
3. a
4. e
5. b
6. d
7. c
8. a
9. e
10. a
11. c
12. d
13. d
14. b
15. e
16. a
17. e
18. c
19. d
20. b
21. b
22. c
23. e
24. b
25. d
26. c
27. c
28. a
29. D (library)
30. B (decided)
31. D (Saturday)
32. X
33. D (queue)
34. B (delighted)
35. A (Excitedly)
36. X
37. B (birthdays – no apostrophe needed)
38. A (Let's – apostrophe required)
39. A (So – capital letter)
40. X
41. A (careful!" – exclamation mark required)
42. C (go," – close speech mark required)
43. D (hill – capital letter not needed)
44. D
45. A
46. A
47. E
48. B
49. E
50. C

Answers to Paper 2C

1. b
2. c
3. e
4. d
5. a
6. c
7. d
8. d
9. d
10. c
11. b
12. a
13. e
14. c
15. e
16. a
17. e
18. a
19. d
20. b
21. e
22. a
23. c
24. b
25. c
26. e
27. a
28. d
29. D (shining)
30. D (family)
31. C (tasty)
32. A (sandwiches)
33. C (picnic)
34. X
35. A (driving)
36. D (chocolate)
37. X
38. A (dug, – comma required)
39. B (herself, – comma required)
40. D (Olive's – apostrophe required)
41. A (Olive – capital letter for proper noun)
42. B (dirty, – comma required for a list)
43. A (When – capital letter at start of sentence)
44. C
45. A
46. C
47. D
48. A
49. D
50. A

Answers to Paper 2D

1. c
2. e
3. d
4. b
5. c
6. a
7. d
8. e
9. a
10. c
11. d
12. b
13. c
14. e
15. b
16. a
17. d
18. a
19. b
20. a
21. d
22. c
23. d
24. c
25. e
26. d
27. a
28. b
29. B (thought)
30. D (sponge)
31. D (liquid)
32. A (quickly)
33. X
34. C (stopped)
35. A (to)
36. B (pail)
37. D (day. – full stop at end of sentence)
38. A (His – capital letter at start of sentence)
39. B (much," – comma required)
40. A (You're – misplaced apostrophe)
41. D (Eastenders – capital letter for proper noun)
42. X
43. B (plants, – comma required for a list)
44. C
45. C
46. E
47. C
48. B
49. D
50. E

Answers to Paper 2E

1. a
2. d
3. c
4. d
5. e
6. e
7. b
8. a
9. b
10. c
11. a
12. e
13. d
14. a
15. b
16. d
17. c
18. a
19. d
20. d
21. a
22. b
23. a
24. c
25. b
26. e
27. d
28. c
29. B (decided)
30. A (which)
31. B (excited)
32. C (disappointed)
33. X
34. C (surprise)
35. D (climbed)
36. A (through)
37. C (Mrs – capital letter required)
38. C (grapes, – comma required for list)
39. D (ideas – apostrophe not required)
40. D (evening. – full stop at end of sentence)
41. X
42. D (phone. – full stop at end of sentence)
43. C (tea?" – question mark required)
44. E
45. B
46. D
47. A
48. A
49. C
50. E

Marking scheme for Compositions

Technical Skills	Marks up to
How well does the story show evidence of a clear beginning, middle and end?	5
How well does the story give a sense of completion?	5
How well has punctuation been used (including paragraphing)?	5
How accurate is the spelling?	5
Overall impression of presentation (neatness, legibility, correction of errors, etc.).	2
Content and Quality	**Marks up to**
How well does the story reflect the requirements of the title given?	5
How well has the candidate used descriptive techniques, e.g., adjectives, adverbs, similes, to enhance the story?	6
How well has direct speech been used and punctuated correctly?	6
How well have the feelings of the character(s) been described?	5
How coherent is the story, i.e., does it flow from beginning to end?	3
Discretionary marks awarded for overall impression of the story's effectiveness	3

Marking scheme for Letters

Technical Skills	Marks up to
Are the address and date placed correctly?	2
Appropriate salutation reflecting the type of letter and person addressed, e.g., Dear Sir/Madam etc.	2
How well does the letter show evidence of a suitable introduction/beginning, middle and end?	4
How well does the letter give a sense of completion?	5
Has the writer signed off the letter in a manner appropriate to the recipient, i.e., in a formal or informal manner?	2
How well has punctuation been used (including paragraphing)?	5
How accurate is the spelling?	5
Overall impression of presentation (neatness, legibility, correction of errors, etc.).	2
Content and Quality	**Marks up to**
How well does the letter reflect the requirements of the title given?	5
How well has the candidate covered the three areas suggested in the task advice?	9 (3 per area)
Is an attempt made to address the recipient using appropriate language, i.e., formal (standard English) or informal (non-standard English)?	3
How coherent is the letter, i.e., does it flow?	3
Discretionary marks for overall impression of the letter's effectiveness in achieving the task set.	3

For more detailed advice and practical help with understanding punctuation, punctuation for direct speech and layout for letter writing and reports, see *Tutor Master helps you Learn English – A Literacy Dictionary*.

www.tutormaster-services.co.uk www.tutormaster-services.co.uk www.tutormaster-services.co.uk www.tutormaster-services.co.uk

Marking scheme for Speech Conversations

Technical Skills	Marks up to
Consistent use of capital letters to begin the words that are spoken.	3
Consistent use of speech marks (" ") to enclose words that are spoken.	3
Consistent use of final pair of speech marks to enclose other punctuation marks, e.g., full stops, exclamation and question marks	3
Consistent use of a new line used for each new speaker.	5
Consistent use of commas to separate words that are spoken from those unspoken.	4
How accurate is the spelling?	5
Overall impression of presentation (neatness, legibility, correction of errors, etc.).	2
Content and Quality	**Marks up to**
How well does the conversation reflect the requirements of the title given?	5
How coherent is the conversation, i.e., does it flow from beginning to end?	3
Does the conversation read/sound realistic?	2
How well does the conversation give a sense of completion?	3
How well have a variety of 'verbs of saying' been used by the speakers, e.g., said, replied, suggested, etc.?	5
How well have adverbs been used to convey the sense of expression of the speaker, e.g., replied happily, spoke sadly?	4
Discretionary marks for overall impression of the conversation's effectiveness in achieving the task set.	3

Marking scheme for Report

Technical Skills	Marks up to
How well does the report show evidence of a clear beginning, middle and end?	5
How well does the report give a sense of completion?	5
How well has punctuation been used (including paragraphing)?	5
How accurate is the spelling?	5
Overall impression of presentation (neatness, legibility, correction of errors, etc.).	2
Content and Quality	**Marks up to**
How well does the report reflect the requirements of the title given?	5
Is there evidence of originality of ideas that goes beyond reflecting the information set out in the reading passage?	5
How well has the candidate covered the three areas suggested in the task advice?	9 (3 per area)
How coherent is the report, i.e., does it flow from beginning to end?	5
Discretionary marks for overall impression of the report's effectiveness in achieving the task set.	4